QUEEN ANNE'S COUNTY MARYLAND

LAND RECORDS

BOOK FOUR: 1743–1755

VOLUMES R.T. C
AND R.T. D

COMPILED BY
R. BERNICE LEONARD

HERITAGE BOOKS
2014

HERITAGE BOOKS
AN IMPRINT OF HERITAGE BOOKS, INC.

Books, CDs, and more—Worldwide

For our listing of thousands of titles see our website
at
www.HeritageBooks.com

Published 2014 by
HERITAGE BOOKS, INC.
Publishing Division
5810 Ruatan Street
Berwyn Heights, Md. 20740

Originally published by R. Bernice Leonard: 1994

International Standard Book Numbers
Paperbound: 978-1-58549-373-9
Clothbound: 978-0-7884-9037-8

QUEEN ANN'S COUNTY LAND RECORDS

CONTENTS - BOOK FOUR

****

ABOUT THE INDEXES

References are to the page numbers of the original records - shown in the left-hand margins of this book.

THE ORIGIN OF QUEEN ANN'S COUNTY

Since Talbot County was the parent of Queen Ann's County, it behooves us to touch briefly on it's origin at the beginning.

The date on which Talbot County was formally established has never come to light; it may have been as early as 1658 when surveyors began to lay out land on the eastern side of the Chesapeake Bay en masse. The name appears with certainty in a charge made by the General Assembly to the interim Sheriff, 18 February 1661. At this time and during the ensuing years, Talbot extended northward to the Chester River and there are evidences that there were tracts on the northern side of the river held by colonists who were under the jurisdiction of the Talbot County court. Poplar Island, lying in the Chesapeake Bay to the westward of Talbot, had been given to Kent (Island) County in 1657 but must have been in the territory laid out for Talbot County, for on 4 June 1671, Philip Calvert ordered that the land on the northeast side of Chester River - "as far as the bounds of Talbot County were formerly - shall now be added to Kent County, as also Poplars Island. And, I do require that the Sheriff of Talbot County not to collect any quit rents from the inhabitants living there." Even so, uncertainty prevailed in some minds, for in a survey made 5 February 1684, for a parcel of land called "Craycroft's Purchase," the tract is described as lying in Talbot County at the head of the Gunpowder River! The eastern border of Talbot, subject of dispute for decades, seems to been acknowledged by those landowners in what is now the First Election District of Queen Ann's County, for as late as 1740, "an old poplar tree - the southwest corner of Governour Penn's Mannor of Pensilvania," was a landmark. In 1695 Kent Island was given to Talbot, a decision of unpopularity to many of the settlers.

Forty-five years after Talbot County had become a part of Maryland history, the settlements along the Chester River, the Tuckahoe and Great Choptank, had grown considerably. The County Courthouse, located at Yorke on a tributary of Wye River called Skipton Creek, was a long journey from Head of Chester (now Millington in Queen Ann's County) and equally so for those plantation owners living east of Tuckahoe Creek on St. Jones' Path (the road from Tuckahoe to St. Jones, now Dover, Delaware). The Governor and Council of the Province were beseiged with petitions from the inhabitants of both Talbot and Kent Counties for a more equitable access to the seat of Justice. So, at the session of Assembly beginning 2 April 1706, the petitions having been read and under consideration for two years, it was decided to divide Talbot County into two parts, the new county so formed to be called QUEEN ANN'S COUNTY, after Queen Anne, consort of King James I of England. Two new courthouses were then needed so commissioners were appointed to arrange for the surveys and purchase of two acres of land for the site of each. That selected for Queen Ann's was on the plantation of John Hawkins on Coursey's Creek; where the county seat was to be called QUEENS TOWN. Here the first county courthouse was erected before 1710.

The Levy List presented at the November 1706 term of Talbot County Court reveals the charges and payments made for the expense of dividing the county. Paid in tobacco at the rate of eighty pounds per day "for canoing to divide ye county," were Daniel Sherwood (3); John Hawkins (3); Richard Tilghman (3); William Turlo (1); Philemon Hemsley (2); Matthew Tilghman Ward (4); John Coppedge (2); William Elliott (2); Valentine Carter (2); William Browne (2); Robert Goldsborough (1). Ralph Stevenson, Innkeeper, received 920 pounds of tobacco "for the expenses of those persons at their first meeting in consulting about dividing ye county."

William Turbutt, Surveyor, was paid 2,500 pounds of tobacco "for running out ye divisional line;" Robert Grundy received 320 "for four days attendance in dividing ye county" and four hundred pounds more "for accomodating all those persons which were about ye same." Chain carriers were paid twenty-five pounds of tobacco per day and Robert Ungle collected 480 pounds "for several chain carriers about ye divisional line;" while the following made claims in person: William Martin (1); William Cooper (4); James London (4); John Hall (1); William Draper (1); David Arey (3); Joseph Arey (3); John Keld (3). At 80 pounds of tobacco per day, John Dawson (2); Thomas Emerson (5); Robert Grundy (2) and James Lloyd (6), were paid "for attendance about dividing ye county."

In the same levy, a payment of 1,200 pounds of tobacco was made to Col. Thomas Smith, Speaker of The House "for a Bill for ye division of Kent and Queen Ann's Counties;" and 600 pounds paid to William Taylard for the same.

Once the divisions were made, the Assembly set the court dates as the first Tuesday in February, April, July, September, October and December. Extant records show sessions of court held in every month in later years. At least two Justices were required to be present during each session, they to have power to determine the length of time needed to conduct the court's business.

The first Clerk of Court for Queen Ann's County was Evan Thomas (E.T.). The second, beginning in 1714, was James Knowles (I.K.); the third was Richard Tilghman (R.T.).

****

BIBLIOGRAPHY

Tavern In The Town - Leonard, 1992
The County Courthouses of Maryland - Radoff, 1960
Queen Anne's County, Maryland - Emory, 1886-7
Old Kent - Hanson, 1876
The Counties of Maryland - Matthews, 1907
Judgments (County Court Records) - Maryland State Archives

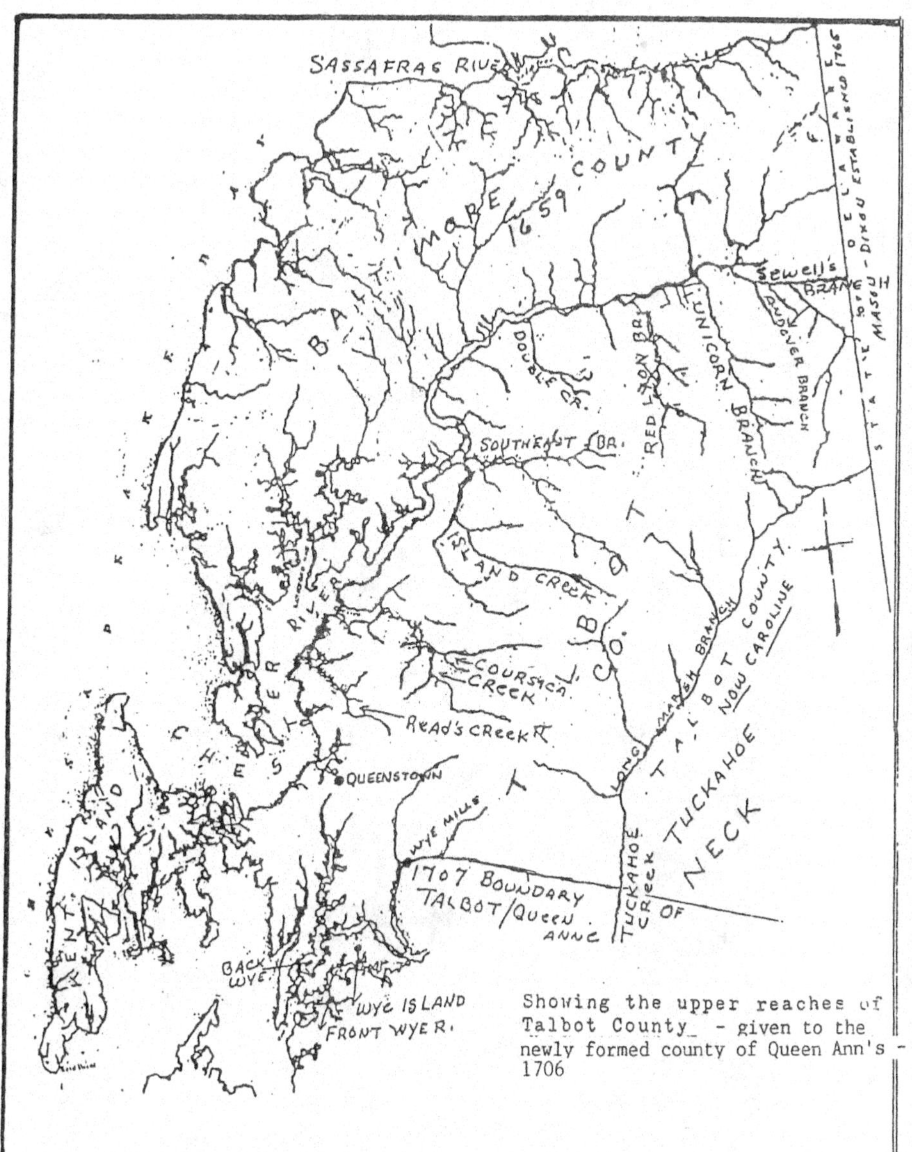

Showing the upper reaches of Talbot County - given to the newly formed county of Queen Ann's - 1706

QUEEN ANNE COUNTY LAND RECORDS - R. T. C 1743 - 1751

Page

266. 27 November 1747 Thomas Loden(?), Sawyer, and Mary his wife, to James Lane, Planter - consideration 5,000 pounds of tobacco - 50 acres on Tuckahoe Creek, part of "Worley's Outrange." Wit: Nathaniel Knotts, Giles Hicks. Thomas and Mary (she being first privately examined out of hearing of her husband) acknowledged before Robert Loyid (sic!) and Associate Justices.

268. 27 November 1747 John Hollingsworth, Innholder, to Ernault Hawkins and Anthony Roe - consideration 3,000 pounds of tobacco - four featherbeds and furniture, one walnut desk, one walnut oval table. Acknowledged before William Tilghman and James Brown, Justices of the Peace.

268. 24 October - 28 November 1747 Anne Ivey of Kent County (Md.), Spinster, to Thomas Harris - consideration ₤12.10.0 - 35 acres, part of "Reason," on the west side of Thomas' Branch - adjoining "Ditteridge," "Stanford" and Seth's millpond. Acknowledged by Anne Ivey and Mary Powell before Charles Downes and William Hopper. Alienation fine, one shilling, five pence sterling paid to Richard Tilghman.

270. 27 October 1747 - 28 November 1747 William Dulaney, Planter, to Thomas Harris, Planter - land called "Stanford" and part of "Mt. Mill," 260 acres mortgaged in 1746 for ₤52.5.0. Lying on the west side of Thomas' Branch, 200 acres adjoining William Young's "Middle Plantation" - also 60 acres, part of "Mt. Mill." Acknowledged before Charles Downes and Nathan Wright. Alienation fine, nine shillings, two pence, half pence sterling.

272. 25 August 1747 - 30 November 1747 Nathan Wright and Ambrose Wright, appointed and sworn to view and value the land called "Upper Deal," the right of Mary and Elizabeth Evans, minors and coheirs (with Anne Price) now under the care of Joseph Evans, their guardian - on 14 July last, entered and found upon the plantation occupied by Alice Wright, widow, one clapboard dwelling house, 20 by 15 feet, wants repair; two small logg houses, not worth repairing; one tobacco house, good rough work, 40 by 20 feet; one old corn house, not worth repairing; one small orchard; the fencing middling good. The guardian permitted to clear twenty acres. On the plantation now occupied by George Bennett, one old dwelling house, 25 by 22 feet; one other dwelling house, 16 by 12 feet, almost new; one tobacco house, 40 by 22 feet, very good; one other tobacco house, 40 by 20 feet, not worth repairing; one cornhouse, wanted repairing; the fencing in good repair; the guardian permitted to clear twenty acres, with liberty to cut timber for necessary repairs. We value two-thirds of the estate at 800 pounds of tobacco per annum. Wit: N. Wright, Jr.

272. 1 December 1747 Benjamin Boon, Planter, to Nathaniel Clow, Planter - consideration 2,100 pounds of tobacco - 50 acres, part of "Boon's

272. Hope," lying on Dickinson's Branch issuing out of Choptank River and near the mouth of Gotherd's Branch. Acknowledged before Charles Downes and William Hopper, Justices of the Peace. Esther, wife of Benjamin Boon, privately examined out of his hearing. Alienation fine, two shillings sterling, paid to Richard Tilghman.

273. 25 August 1747 - 2 December 1747 Samuel Massey of Chester Town, Hatter, to John Haymer - consideration ₤100 current money and 8,000 pounds of tobacco - 300 acres called "Chestnut Neck" - on Dividing Creek of Chester River - adjoining "Poplar Hill" and Fishing Creek. Acknowledged in Kent County (Md.) before Charles Hynson and Bedingfield Hands, certified by James Smith, Clerk of Kent County.

274. 2 December 1747 Nathaniel Wright and Ambrose Wright, appointed and sworn to view and value the land called "Upper Deal," the right of Ann Price being one-third, coheir with Mary and Elizabeth Evans - Joseph Evans, guardian of Ann Price, a minor. (see page 272)

275. 1 December 1747 William Burch, Planter, to John Collins - one bay mare, one brindle cow and calf. Wit: John Offley Collins, Samuel French.

275. 19 July 1747 - 2 December 1747 John Hawkins, Planter, and Sarah his wife, to Robert Hawkins, Planter - consideration 25,000 pounds of tobacco and ₤25 currency - 400 acres, part of "Macklinborough" and "Tulley's Delight" - beginning at the northernmost corner of a lot in Ogletown formerly belonging to William Meredith, on the road leading from Ogletown out of the neck - adjoining a part of "Macklinborough" lately in possession of John Cheares and a part owned by Edward Brown - running to a lot in Ogletown belonging to Matthew Dockwra. John and Sarah (she being first privately examined) acknowledged before Nathaniel Wright, Jr. and William Clayton.

277. 2 December 1747 Thomas Purnall of Talbot County, Planter; Abraham Boon and Joseph Boon of Queen Anne County, Planters, to William Banckes, Merchant - consideration 5,400 pounds of tobacco and the sum of ₤3.2.4 current money - 500 acres called "Partnership," on the eastern branch of Choptank River. Acknowledged before James Brown and Jonathon Nicols. Alienation fine, twenty shillings sterling.

279. 19 December 1747 - 24 December 1747 Joseph Maugridge, Weaver, to Thomas Stephens, Planter - consideration 4,140 pounds of tobacco - two bay horses about seven years old; one bay colt; three cows and yearlings; one heafer (sic!) with calf; three sows; fifteen shoats; one featherbed and furniture. Wit: Thomas Wilkinson, Thomas Wilkinson, Jr. Acknowledged before Nathan Wright.

279. 26 December 1747 Joseph Elliott and Cornelius Comegys, appointed and sworn by Humphrey Wells, Jr. to view and value the plantation of Bexley John Lambdin, a minor, who has lately made choice of James Hobbs for his guardian; the son and heir of George Lambdin, deceased who died possessed of "Lambden's Adventure," containing 100 acres -

279. entered upon the plantation and found one dwelling house, 25 feet long, shedded on one side, old and out of repair and thirty loose planks lying on the joice; one old kitchen, very much out of repair; one tobacco house, framed, shedded on one side in middling good repair; one corn house in good repair; one old tobacco house, shedded on two sides but very much gone to wrack; one dwelling house on the north end of the plantation, 20 by 15 feet in indifferent order; one small round logged house, 12 by 10 feet, in good order; one old corn house, 15 by 6 feet, very sorry; 150 apple trees and a little nursery of apple trees; 16 cherry trees and 4 pare(sic!) trees; a few old shrubby peach trees; 1,560 pannells of fencing, generally about nine rails high but out of repair; very little woodland. Annual value judged to be 300 pounds of tobacco yearly; Hobbs not to clear more than one-half acre per year.

280. 7 January 1747 Peter Rich and Susanna his wife of Dorsetshere County, Innholders, to their daughter Sidney Herrington of Queen Anne, heirs and husband Nathan during his life; with reversion to our daughter Elizabeth Andrew if Sidney should die without lawful issue - one moiety of "Ingram's Desire," excepting a parcel sold to William Andrew - about fifteen acres and a reserve of about three or four acres on the south side of the road from Choptank Bridge to Tuckahoe Bridge. Wit: Richard Tilghman Earle, John Clothier. Peter and Susanna (she being first privately examined) acknowledged before Richard Tilghman. Alienation fine, four shillings sterling.

281. 14 January 1747 James Millis, Planter, to Thomas Baggs, Planter - consideration 2,000 pounds of tobacco and two shillings sterling - 50 acres, "Chance Hitt," near Oldtown and on the west side of Lowe's Branch. Wit: Henry Councell. Acknowledged before Charles Downes and Edward Tilghman. Alienation fine, two shillings sterling, paid to Richard Tilghman.

281. 6 August 1747 - 14 January 1747 John Parsons and Catherine his wife, to Jacob Alquier - consideration 11,020 pounds of tobacco - 115 acres on Beckles' Creek, south side Chester River - adjoining "Tilghman's Discovery." Acknowledged before James Brown and Humphery Wells. Catherine Parsons examined out of hearing of her husband. Alienation fine, four shillings, seven pence, one farthing.

283. 14 January 1747 Edward Jumpe, Planter, to William Banckes, Merchant - consideration ₤16.13.0 current money - 50 acres, part of "Godfrey's Folly" - in Tuckahoe Neck on the east side of the main branch adjoining "New Buckby," formerly laid out for John Wootters of Talbot County. Acknowledged before William Tilghman and Charles Downes. Alienation fine, two shillings sterling.

284. 10 October 1747 - 27 January 1747 George Lewis, Planter, to Thomas Hammond - consideration ₤20 current - 60 acres of land, part of "Boaquely," on the south side of Coursica Creek - adjoining Esquire Bennett's formerly John Lewis' part and part sold to Richard Tilghman. Originally granted to John Boage for 350 acres and assigned to

284. William Burgess of Annarandel County who assigned it to Thomas and John Lewis and their heirs and divided between them. Thomas Lewis bequeathed his part to his son Thomas who departed this life intestate and the land became the right of his eldest son, George Lewis. Wit: Thomas Chaires, Catherine Chaires. Sarah, wife of George Lewis, acknowledged before Edward Tilghman and William Hopper, J. P.'s.

285. 28 January 1747 James Lloyd, Commander of the ship "Creighton," anchored in the Wye River and bound for London, will take tobacco on board at the rate of ₤16 sterling consigned to James Buchanon, Merchant. NB: The ship's cargo is insured at ₤4 sterling per hogshead.

286. 23 September 1747 - 1 February 1747 Samuel Massey of Chestertown, Kent County, Hatter, and Sarah his wife, to James Auld of Dorchester County - consideration ₤5 current - Lot #19 in Kings Town on Chester River. Acknowledged before Henry Hooper and Robert Jenkins Henry, Justices of the Orovincial Court. Sarah being first privately examined.

287. 27 January 1747 - 4 February 1747 Elizabeth Baynard, Widow, to her son Joshua Clarke - a gift of love - negro boy named "Stepne" and a featherbed valued at ₤8 current. Acknowledged before Jonathon Nicols and witnessed by Mary Small.

287. 27 January 1747 - 4 February 1747 Elizabeth Baynard to her daughter, Lydia Clarke - gift of a negro girl named "Dafany" and one featherbed valued at ₤8 current. Wit: Mary Small. Acknowledged before Jonathon Nicols.

288. 22 January 1747 - 18 February 1747 James Lihon of the Island of Guernsey within the territories of Great Britain, brother and heir of Thomas Lihon, late of the same Island, Marriner - by John Connor, his attorney, to John Hollingsworth, Innholder - consideration ₤10.11.0 current - Lot #3 in Kings Town. Acknowledged before Bedingfield Hands and W. Harris, Justices of the Peace for Kent County (Md.). Certified by James Smith, Clerk for Kent County.

289. 23 January 1747 Sarah Hart, Widow, to her daughter, Ann Johnson - a gift of love - negro man named "Dick," a negro boy named "Sam," about three years, a negro girl named "Daphne," about two months, one good featherbed and all furniture, two cows, four sheep, a gelding riding horse called "Blackey," two iron pots, one frying pan, one iron skillet, one looking glass, one box iron and heaters, one ovall walnut table, four pewter dishes, twelve pewter plates, three chaires, one leather trunk, one silver soope spoon and four silver teaspoons, two gold rings, one chest, one wood table, two earthen punch bowls, three earthen plates, one woman's saddle and bridle. Further, after my decease, a negro woman named "Jenny," about twenty five. 22 January 1747. Wit: John Loockerman, Jr. and Thomas Clark.

290. 24 October 1747 - 25 February 1747 Anne Ivey and Mary Powell of Kent County (Md.), seamster, to John Welch, Planter - consideration 2,000

290. pounds of tobacco - 20 acres, part of "Reason," on the west side of Thomas' Branch - adjoining the land of old Thomas Harris and William Campbell, part of "Ditteridge." Acknowledged before Charles Downes and William Hopper.

291. 25 February 1747 Richard Tilghman, Gentleman, oldest son and heir of Richard Tilghman, Esquire, deceased, to Edward Tilghman, a son - reference made to Richard Tilghman's will dated 25 April 1737 - 239 acres on Unicorn Branch called "Malten." Acknowledged before William Tilghman and William Hopper.

292. 3 March 1747 Stephen Thomas to Trustrum Thomas - consideration 1,500 pounds of tobacco - part of "Trustrum," surplus land as determined by commissioners Robert Lloyd and Nathan Wright. Stephen and Mary his wife (she being first privately examined) acknowledged before Robert Lloyd and William Hopper. Alienation fine, one shilling two pence sterling, paid to Richard Tilghman.

293. 5 January 1747 - 10 March 1747 William Carman, Planter, and Margaret his wife, to Thomas Hackett, Planter - consideration ₺30 current money - 50 acres, part of "Shetland" - on Broadrib's Creek. William and Margaret (she being first privately examined) acknowledged before James Brown and Nathan Wright.

294. 24 October 1747 - 23 March 1747 Anne Ivey of Kent County (Md.), Spinster, heir at law of Robert Smith to Nathan Wright - consideration 2,500 pounds of tobacco - 34 acres, part of "Smith's Reserve" - lying on the west side of the part sold to Thomas Obryon and adjoining "Pleasant Spring." Anne Ivey and Mary Powell acknowledged their deed before Charles Downes and William Hopper. Alienation fine, two shillings, four pence half penny sterling paid to R. Tilghman.

296. 23 March 1747 - 24 March 1747 Thomas Porter, Planter, and Mary his wife, to Hawkins Downes, Planter - consideration 4,000 pounds of tobacco and ₺30 current - 100 acres, part of "Porter's Folly" - near "Colerain." Thomas and Mary (she being first privately examined) acknowledged before Charles Downes and William Hopper. Alienation fine, four shillings sterling.

297. 14 October 1747 - 24 March 1747 William Coursey, Gentleman, to his daughter, Rachel Coursey - gift of a negro named "Nann," with all of her issue. Acknowledged before Edward Tilghman.

297. 18 February 1747 - 24 March 1747 Samuel Massey of Kent County (Md.) to Daniel Bird of Bideford in Great Britain, Marriner - consideration ₺5 current - Lot #8 in Kings Town. Acknowledged before James Brown and Humphrey Wells, Jr., Justices.

298. 2 March 1747 - 25 March 1747 John McConekin, Planter, and Mary his wife, to William Wilson, Planter - consideration ₺320 paper currency - part of "Woodridge," 184 acres and part of "McConakin's Fortune," 143 acres - near Wallis'es Marsh. John and Mary acknowledged

298. before Robert Lloyd and Edward Tilghman. Mary being first privately examined out of hearing of her husband.

300. 24 December 1747 Nathaniel Knotts and William Fisher, appointed and sworn before Jonathan Nicols to view and value the land of Daniel Dulaney - found one dwelling house, lapt work, 20 by 15 feet, a like covering; one 30 by 20 feet tobacco house, wanting covering; all the clair (sic!) ground inclosed with fence and rales (sic!) to a panel four. The annual rent 300 pounds of tobacco - the guardian or tenant to cut timber as needed.

301. 26 March 1748 Mary Scotten, Widow, to Joseph Elliott, Planter - consideration ₤30.10.0 - 100 acres, part of "Salisbury Plains" - lying on the east side of the main branch of Choptank River. Acknowledged before Humphrey Wells, Jr. and William Hopper. Alienation fine, four shillings sterling paid to Richard Tilghman.

303. 18 February 1747 - 16 April 1748 Samuel Massey of Chester Town in Kent County (Md.) to Mary Williams of the same place, Widow - consideration ₤5 - Lot #17 in Kings Town. Wit: James Brown, Charles Peale. Acknowledged before Humphrey Wells, Jr. and James Brown.

303. 23 March 1747 - 20 April 1748 Benjamin Jumpe, son of William, Planter, and Hannah his wife, to William Banckes, Merchant - consideration ₤40 current and 1,000 pounds of tobacco - 126 acres, part of "Pokety Ridge" and "Jump's Chance" - on the north side of the main road leading from Tuckahoe Bridge to the head of Choptank - adjoining Thomas Jump's land. Benjamin and Hannah (she being first privately examined) acknowledged before James Brown and Humphrey Wells, Jr.

305. 23 March 1747 - 20 April 1848 William Colvin to Alexander Tolson - consideration 7,000 pounds of tobacco - 140 acres, part of "Freshford" that William Colvin lately dwelled on, which formerly belonged to William Hambleton. Lying on Elliott's Branch of Island Creek. William and Elizabeth his wife (she being first privately examined) acknowledged before Robert Lloyd and William Hopper. Alienation fine, five shillings, seven pence half penny sterling.

306. 30 March 1748 - 20 April 1748 Michael Earle of Cecil County, Gentleman, heir of James Earle of Queen Anne, Gentleman, deceased, to Richard Tilghman, Gentleman - consideration five shillings - moiety of "Sprigley" excluded from a deed made between James Earle, father of Michael Earle, to Richard Tilghman, Sr. father of Richard Tilghman, 7 January 1717. Acknowledged before John Baldwin and John Veasey, Justices of the Peace for Cecil County; certified by Francis Lee, Clerk of Cecil County.

307. 14 January 1746 - 20 April 1748 William Diggs of Prince George's County, Gentleman, to Richard Bennett, Esquire - consideration 18,600 pounds of tobacco - 186 acres, part of "Branford" - adjoining the second line of Stephen Yoe's part of the said land and the

307. part sold to John Mead and the land called "St. Martin's." Wit: John Darnall, John Thompson. Acknowledged before John Darnall, a Justice of the Provincial Court.

308. 15 March 1747 - 21 April 1748 Archibald Greenfield, Marriner, to Thomas Bryant, Planter - consideration ₤80 current - Lots #2, #22, "35, "38, "39, "41, "44 and "59, with all improvements - in Ogletown. Wit: Thomas Clark, Samuel Massey. Acknowledged before Thomas Bordley and Charles Scott, Justices of the Peace for Kent County (Md.). Certified by James Smith, Clerk of Kent County. Alienation fine, six pence sterling paid to Richard Tilghman.

309. 5 April 1748 - 22 April 1748 Ernault Hawkins, Planter, and Jane his wife, to Edward Tilghman, Gentleman - consideration ₤4 lawful paper money of Maryland and 2,300 pounds of tobacco - 100 acres called "Rear Guard," situated in Queen Anne County (this formerly in Kent County) - adjoining "Forlorn Hope," near Sewell's Branch of Chester River. Ernault and Jane (she being first privately examined) acknowledged before William Hopper and Nathan Wright. Alienation fine, four shillings sterling.

310. 30 April 1748 - 5 May 1748 John Harding, Planter, to Fardinando Callaghane and John Kiningmont, Planters - two cows; one pide heipher (sic!); one pide stear earling (sic!); one young calf; two ewes and lambs; one young iron gray horse - worth 2,000 pounds of tobacco for the cost of security of the cost of a sale brought by Foster Cunliffe & Sons against John Harding.

311. 26 April 1748 - 5 May 1748 Anne Ivey of Kent County (Md.), heir at law of Robert Smith, Esquire, deceased, to Richard Tilghman - consideration ₤5.12.6 - part of "Confusion," adjoining a part sold by Anthony Ivey and Anne his wife to John Alla - containing 9 acres. Wit: James Ringgold, Jr. and Thomas Ringgold. Acknowledged before Robert Jenckins Henry, Justice of the Provincial Court.

311. 26 April 1748 - 5 May 1748 Mary Powell of Kent County (Md.), lately the widow of Robert Ivey, but now widow of Nehemiah Powell, and Anne Ivey, daughter of Robert Ivey and heir at law of Robert Smith, Esquire, to Richard Tilghman Earle, Gentleman - consideration 2,500 pounds of tobacco and ₤5 current money - "Adventure," lying in the branches of Coursica Creek - adjoining a tract formerly laid out for William Hemsley - excepting for such parts already sold. Wit: James Rigby, Jr., Thomas Ringgold. Acknowledged before Robert Jenckins Henry, Justice of the Provincial Court.

312. 1 April 1748 - 5 May 1748 Vincent Lowe of Talbot County, Planter, to William Knotts, Planter - consideration 7,000 pounds of tobacco - 116 acres, part of "The Beginning," lying on the north side of the Unicorn Branch. Acknowledged before James Brown and Humphrey Wells, Jr. Alienation fine, four shillings, eight pence sterling.

313. 1 April 1748 - 5 May 1748 Vincent Lowe of Talbot County, Planter,

313. to John Hartshorne, Carpenter - consideration 7,000 pounds of tobacco - 150 acres, part of "The Addition," lying on the north side of the Unicorn Branch. Acknowledged before James Brown and Humphrey Wells, Jr.

315. 1 April 1748 - 5 May 1748 Vincent Lowe of Talbot County, Planter, to Robert Certain, Jr., Planter - consideration 7,000 pounds of tobacco - 116 acres, part of "The Beginning," on the north side of the Unicorne Branch. Acknowledged before James Brown and Humphrey Wells, Jr. Alienation fine, four shillings, eight pence sterling, paid to Richard Tilghman.

316. 27 April 1748 - 6 May 1748 Richard Wells, Yoeman, to Richard Wells, Jr. of Dover, County of Kent, Delaware, Surgeon - consideration ₤28 sterling money of Great Britain - 100 acres, part of "Bath," that my brother Humphrey Wells now lives on; and the remaining part of "Bath's Addition," adjoining and containing 100 acres of land. Acknowledged before James Brown and Humphrey Wells, Jr. Alienation fine, six shillings sterling, paid to Richard Tilghman.

317. 27 April 1748 - 6 May 1748 Mary Powell of Kent County (Md.), Widow, and Anne Ivey, daughter of Robert Ivey, deceased and heir at law to Robert Smith, deceased, to John Jackson, Physician - consideration 3,000 pounds of tobacco - 200 acres, "Smithfield" - lying formerly in Talbot County but by the late division now in Queen Anne County on the east side of Fishing Creek Branch of Chester River. Wit: Henry Hooper, James Tilghman. Receipt to Dr. Jackson witnessed by Robert Lloyd and James Hollyday. Acknowledged before Henry Hooper, Justice of the Provincial Court. Alienation fine, four shillings sterling.

318. 5 May 1748 - 9 June 1748 Edward Godwin, Planter, and Mary his wife to Nathan Wright - consideration ₤15 sterling - 100 acres, all of "Long Run," adjoining Thomas Todd. Edward and Mary (she being first privately examined) acknowledged before James Brown and William Hopper. Alienation fine, four shillings sterling.

319. 7 May 1748 - 9 June 1748 William Hopper, Gentleman, to Matthew Dockery, Innholder - leases his grist mill, commonly called Chester Mill (with the ten acres of land thereto belonging); with liberty of cutting timber and wood for fencing on "Chesterfield" for the use of the mill and houses on the said land. Also all that plantation adjoining to the mill land on the north side, part of "Chesterfield," beginning at a beech tree standing below the mill house and running south, then east to "Fishingham Addition;" then to "Fishingham," and the main road leading from William Hopper's gate to Chester Mill, then across the road to the head of the Spring Valley - for a term of fifteen years. Acknowledged before James Brown and Humphrey Wells, Jr.

320. 30 December 1747 - 10 June 1748 Daniel Newnam of Kent County on Delaware, Planter, and Sarah his wife, to John Seegar, Mariner -

320. consideration £200 current - 241½ acres, "Newnam's Portion," adjoining "Sledmore" now in possession of Capt. Joseph Sudler and Daniel Newnam's part of "Devonishes Chance." Daniel and Sarah (she being first privately examined) acknowledged before James Brown and Humphrey Wells, Jr. Alienation fine, nine shillings, eight pence sterling paid to Richard Tilghman.

323. 5 April 1748 - 16 June 1748 Thomas Godwin, Planter, to Thomas Robinson, Planter and Hannah his wife - consideration £50 current - 100 acres, part of "Wright's Choice," on the north side of the southeast branch of Island Creek - adjoining "Smith's Range." Also for love and affection towards Hannah Robinson and the further sum of five shillings, all of his personal estate whatsoever. Acknowledged before James Brown and Nathan Wright. Alienation fine, four shillings sterling.

324. 9 June 1748 - 28 June 1748 Zorababel Wells to Richard Wells, Jr. of Dover, Kent County on Delaware - consideration 3,000 pounds of tobacco and £15 current - 50 acres, part of "Bath's Addition," conveyed to Zorababel by his father Richard Wells of Queen Anne County, 11 May 1743. Acknowledged before James Brown and Humphrey Wells, Jr. Alienation fine, two shillings sterling.

325. 18 February 1747 - 28 June 1748 James Read, Weaver, to William Taylor of Kent County (Md.), Shoemaker - consideration £5 - lot #12 in Ogle Town. James and Mary his wife, (she being first privately examined) acknowledged before James Brown and Humphrey Wells, Jr. Alienation fine, three farthings sterling.

326. 25 June 1748 - 28 June 1748 Peter Massey, Carpenter, and Mary his wife, to John Seegar, Marriner - consideration £55 current - 100 acres called "Johnson's Adventure," near the Unicorne Branch and adjoining Simon Wilmer's land. Peter and Mary (she being first privately examined out of his hearing) acknowledged before James Brown and Humphrey Wells, Jr. Alienation fine, four shillings sterling.

327. 28 July 1748 Thomas Stanton, Planter, to Peter Rich of Dorchester County, Innholder - consideration 1,500 pounds of tobacco - a lot in Bridgetown known as "Stanton's Lott" - being ye lott my father, John Stanton, took up and built on as ye law directed. Acknowledged before James Brown and Joseph Sudler. Alienation fine, three shillings sterling.

328. 11 May 1748 - 28 July 1748 William Elliott, Planter, to Samuel Osburn, Planter - consideration five shillings - 200 acres called "Addition" on Kent Island near the Alder Swamp and Long Creek - a lease for one year. Witnessed by the people then on the land: Joseph Derochbrune, Sr., Lewis Derochbrune, Sr., Joseph Derochbrune, Jr., Lewis Derochbrune, Jr., John Derochbrune and William Derochbrune. Acknowledged before Robert Lloyd and his Associate Justices. Richard Tilghman, Clerk of Queen Anne County.

329. 12 May 1748 - 28 July 1748 William Elliott, Planter, to Samuel Osburn, Planter - consideration 20,000 pounds of tobacco - 200 acres called the "Addition," on Kent Island. Wit: Matthew Griffith, William Baxter, James Hutchings, Thomas Benton. Acknowledged before Robert Lloyd and Associates. Alienation fine, fourteen shillings sterling, paid to Richard Tilghman.

330. 18 February 1748 - 4 August 1748 John Hollingsworth, Innholder, to William Dames of Chester Town, Merchant - consideration £60 current money - lott #3 in Kings Town, John and Elizabeth his wife (she being first privately examined) acknowledged before James Brown and Humphrey Wells, Jr.

331. 9 March 1747 - 4 August 1748 John Haymer, Planter, and Sarah Firth, Widow, to William Dames, Merchant - consideration £200 current and 12,000 pounds of tobacco - 300 acres called "Chestnut Neck" near Kings Town and Dividing Creek - adjoining "Poplar Hill," William Henecy's parcel and Quicksand Marsh - on Chester River. Acknowledged before James Brown and Humphrey Wells, Jr. A receipt given to Dames was signed "John Hamer, Jr."

332. 1 August 1748 - 16 August 1748 Thomas Cooper, Planter, and Amelia his wife, to Henry Jacobs, Planter - consideration £100 current - the lot whereon he lately liveth in Queens Town, on the south side of the lot of Col. Richard Tilghman. Acknowledged before James Brown and Humphrey Wells, Jr.

333. 10 August 1748 - 18 August 1748 William Cooper, Planter, to Sharpless Cooper, Planter, his son - a gift of love with further consideration of £5 current money - all of "Hill's Outlet" in Tuckahoe Neck. Acknowledged before Edward Tilghman and Jonathon Nicols. Alienation fine, four shillings sterling paid to Richard Tilghman.

334. 15 August 1748 - 24 August 1748 William Carmichall and John Hackett appointed and sworn to make an estimate of the value of the land belonging to Richard Cook, an orphan - entered upon the land and found 335 acres in one tract under a good fence, on which is one dwelling house, 40 by 16 feet with two wooden chimneys, wanting a loft and some small repair. One new house, intended for a kitchen, without a loft, doors, windows or a chimney; one log house, 12 by 10 feet; one hen house, 16 by 10 feet; a log barn, 24 by 16 feet with sheds and a shingled roof; one tobacco house, 40 by 22 feet, covered with boards, a bastard frame much out of repair; one brick shed; one old log cornhouse, 16 by 10 feet. Six acres may be cleared yearly on the east side of the plantation; the annual value 750 pounds of tobacco. Also an orchard of 70 young apple trees and 31 cherry trees.

334. 6 August 1748 - 25 August 1748 Matthew Dockery, Innholder, to Christopher Cox, Merchant - lease of land for a sufficient cart road from "Cox'es Necessity," lately taken up by Christopher Cos and lying upon a point near Thomas Carradine's plantation on Corsica Creek, the said cart road to run from "Cox'es Necessity" through any part

334. of "Matthew's Fancy" (belonging to Matthew Dockery) to the usual landing that now is or shall be on "Matthew's Fancy" for a term of ninety-nine years, paying one sound ear of Indian corn 1 January when demanded. Acknowledged before William Hopper and Nathan Wright.

335. 13 August 1748 - 25 August 1748 Francis Rochester and Joseph Elliott, appointed and sworn by Humphery Wells, Jr. to view and value the plantation of Christopher Williams, a minor (son and heir of Christopher Williams, deceased), to whom Mr. Jervis Spencer was lately appointed guardian, a tract called "Conaway" of 111 acres - entered upon the land and found one dwelling house, logged walls and plank Floors about 24 by 18 feet in good repair; one citchen (sic!), loggs, 20 by 16 in poor repair; one small logg'd house, 16 by 15 in poor order; one logg'd cornhouse, about 12 by 7 feet in middling order; an old brick oven and about 630 pannells of fencing, about 550 pannells about eight rails high and 80 pannells about seven rails high. The guardian is not to clear more than ten acres in any one year and on the west side of the mill. The annual value, 500 pounds of tobacco.

336. 26 August 1748 Edward Harding, Sr. of Talbot County, Planter, to James Callaghane, Planter - consideration 5,000 pounds of tobacco and ₤6 currency - 70 acres, part of "Arcadia," adjoining "Lambeth." Acknowledged before Humphrey Wells, Jr. and William Hopper. Alienation fine, two shillings sterling paid to Richard Tilghman.

337. 23 July 1748 - 25 August 1748 - Samuel Dickenson of Kent County on Delaware, Province of Pennsylvania, Gentleman, and Henry Dickenson of Talbot County, Province of Maryland, to Robert Hardcastle - consideration 12,000 pounds of tobacco - 150 acres called "Mt. Hope," in Queen Anne County on the west side of Great Choptank River. John Emory of Queen Anne, Gentleman, attorney for Samuel Dickenson. Witnessed by Levin Hull and Charles Goldsborough (who swore to witnessing the deed before Humphrey Wells, Jr. and Nathan Wright, 28 July 1748). Henry Dickenson acknowledged before William Thomas and Thomas Bullen, Justices of Talbot County Court, 4 August 1748. Certified by John Leeds, Clerk of Talbot County.

338. 25 August 1748 - 1 September 1748 Thomas Butler, Planter, to Charles Brown, Merchant - consideration 3,049 pounds of tobacco - one negro girl slave named "Eve" - a mortgage due 1 June next. Wit: James Calder, John Ewing. Acknowledged before Richard Tilghman, a Justice of the Provincial Court.

339. 23 September 1748 Thomas Glentworth, Master of the Snow "Hereford," now lying in Chester (River) and from there bound to Bristole in Great Britain, will take on board tobacco; the freight, ₤8 sterling per tonn, consigned to Daniel Cheston, Merchant.

339. 14 September 1748 - 24 September 1748 Nicholas Broadaway, Planter, to Dr. Richard Porter, Jr. - consideration 7,000 pounds of tobacco - 60 acres, part of "Annthorpe," at Wills Hole - adjoining "Churnell's

339. Neck" and "White Hall." Acknowledged before Robert Lloyd and William Tilghman. Alienation fine, one shilling, two pence, farthing sterling, paid to Richard Tilghman.

340. 29 September 1748 Thomas Beley, Commander of the ship "Allen," now riding at anchor in Wye River, bound for London, will take tobacco on freight at £7 sterling per tonn with liberty of consignments.

340. 9 June 1748 - 23 November 1748 William Hennecy, Carpenter, and his wife Elizabeth, daughter and devisee of John Haymer, deceased, to Samuel Massey of Kent County (Md.), Hatter - consideration £21 current money - 50 acres, part of "Chestnut Neck" - opposite to Chester Town - on Fishing Creek and adjoining "Poplar Hill." William and Elizabeth (she being first privately examined out of his hearing) acknowledged before James Brown and Humphrey Wells, Jr. Alienation fine, two shillings sterling. Signed "William Henissey."

341. 14 November 1748 John Alley, Planter, to Richard Tilghman, Esquire - 110 acres, part of "Confusion" and the "Adventure" on Coursica Creek. Reference made to a Writ of Entry executed in October last. Wit: Richard Tilghman Earle, Richard Keiran.

342. 23 November 1748 John Forbush, Planter, in consideration of the sum of 650 pounds of tobacco and £3 current money, the cost of suit of two actions brought against me by Jervis Spencer and William Hall, to be paid by Richard Tilghman - conveys to Tilghman two cows, one calf, a two-year old heifer, twenty young hoggs, a small sorrel horse and all the fodder on the plantation I now live on. A chattel mortgage due 10 June next. Wit: Richard Tilghman Earle, Henry Johnson. Acknowledged before William Tilghman.

342. 25 November 1748 Joseph Hunter, Planter, to Thomas Baggs - consideration £5 sterling - 50 acres, "Hunter's Hope," lying near Lowe's Marsh. Hunter's receipt to Thomas Baggs witnessed by James Tilghman, Philemon Hemsley and John Clothier. Joseph and Mary his wife (she being first privately examined) acknowledged before Robert Lloyd and his Associates. Alienation fine, two shillings sterling.

343. 25 October 1748 - 30 November 1748 Hynson Wright, Planter, to Ambrose Wright, Planter - consideration 4,000 pounds of tobacco - 52 acres, part of "Guilford," adjoining "Smith's Forrest," now possessed by Ambrose Wright. Hynson and Sarah his wife (she being first privately examined) acknowledged before William Hopper and Nathan Wright. Alienation fine, two shillings, one pence sterling.

344. 3 November 1748 - 30 November 1748 Peter Hinsely, Planter, to Edward Roe - consideration 11,003 pounds of tobacco and £3 paper and eleven shillings sterling money of Great Britain - 100 acres in Tully's Neck called "Hinsely's Choice," adjoining "Oaken Throph (sic!)" and also 40 acres, part of "Oaken Thoph (sic!)." Acknowledged before William Hopper and Nathan Wright.

346. 3 December 1748 - 5 December 1748 John Coursey, Planter, to Richard Bennett, Merchant - consideration ₺368.18.6 sterling money of Great Britain; ₺730.4.2 current money of Maryland and 15,789 pounds of tobacco - "Coursey's Range," originally surveyed for Col. Henry Coursey for 600 acres - also part of "Hemsley's Britland Rectified," resurveyed for Thomas Hynson Wright - conveyed by him to John Coursey for 223 acres. Wit: Thomas Clarke, John Loockerman, Jr. Acknowledged before Richard Tilghman. Alienation fine, twenty shillings, eleven pence, half penny sterling.

347. 19 December 1748 Richard Tilghman, Gentleman, to Edward Tilghman - in compliance with the desire of Anna Maria Tilghman, deceased, mother of Richard and Edward and whose heir at law the said Richard is, and in further consideration of five shillings - 770 acres, "The Union," "Bocking als Bockeing," and "Rosseth," on Thomas' Branch, near the dwelling house where William Clayton late of Queen Anne County did live - which includes "Bocking" and "Rosseth." Richard and Susanna his wife (she being first privately examined out of his hearing) acknowledged before Robert Lloyd and William Tilghman. Alienation fine, ₺1.10.10 sterling.

348. 28 December 1748 Richard Porter, Jr., Chyrurgeon, to Edward Tilghman - consideration ₺100 paper currency of Maryland - the following slaves: "Phillis, about 22, ₺35 paper; "Chester," about 13, ₺30 paper; "Phillis," about 12, ₺20 paper; "Daphny," about 5, ₺10 paper; "Joseph," about 5, ₺5 paper. A chattel mortgage dued on or before 10 April 1749. Wit: Richard Tilghman, Richard Tilghman Earle.

349. 19 December 1748 - 5 January 1748 William Digges to Richard Bennett - a clear title to 186 acres of land called part of "Branford," by mistake called "Brandford" in the deed dated 14 January 1746. Wit: B. Young, Henry Rozer.

350. 28 January 1748 - 30 January 1748 Edward Roe, Planter, to Samuel Roe and Anne his wife - a gift of love to Samuel for his natural life and Anne during her widowhood - 164 acres, part of "Okenthorpe" - lying in the freshes of Tuckahoe Creek, adjoining a part conveyed to John Miller; "Wright's Chance," now in possession of Nathaniel Wright; and "Tully's Addition," now possessed by Edward Roe. Acknowledged before William Hopper and Nathan Wright. Alienation fine, six shillings, seven pence sterling paid to Richard Tilghman.

351. 28 January 1748 - 30 Janaury 1748 Edward Roe to John Row, his son - a gift of love - 150 acres, part of "Narborough." Acknowledged before William Hopper and Nathan Wright. Alienation fine, six shillings sterling.

352. 24 January 1748 - 2 February 1748 Morris Clock's deposition regarding the bounds of the land now in possession of Thomas Roe, which was formerly John Roe's, his father. "He was a servant to Capt. Nathaniel Wright about forty-four years ago and his master set him to work to make a calf pasture in the woods and he cut down a bounded tree

352. for rails - later he went to work for Mr. William Sweatnam who sold land to John Roe, where he had cut the tree" - now shows the stump. Wit: Edward Roe, Nathaniel Wright, William Wilkinson, Thomas Wilkinson, Jr., James Carman. Also written "Mauris Cloack."

353. 2 February 1748 Thomas Price to his son, Thomas Price, Jr. - a gift of love - 64 acres, part of "Conclusion" (out of 150 acres) and 23 acres adjoining, part of the land I now dwell on called "Brandford." Acknowledged before William Hopper and Nathaniel Wright. Alienation fine, three shillings, six pence sterling paid to Richard Tilghman.

353. 3 September 1748 - 2 February 1748 Nathan Samuel Turbutt Wright and Thomas Wright, executors of the will of Thomas Hynson Wright, deceased, to James Reid -in consideration of the sum of ₤27.17.6 current money paid to Thomas Hynson Wright during his lifetime and further consideration of ₤12.2.6 paid to the grantors - 50 acres, part of "Providence" - on the road to Kings Town. Acknowledged before William Hopper and Nathaniel Wright. Alienation fine, two shillings sterling.

355. 4 February 1748 - 7 February 1748 John Davis, Jr., Planter, and Esther his wife, to Robert Cooper of Worcester County, Planter - consideration ₤22 Maryland currency - 32 acres, part of "Peale Place," near the head of Beaverdam Branch of Choptank River. Acknowledged before William Hopper and Nathaniel Wright. Alienation fine, one shilling, three pence, half penny sterling.

356. 25 October 1748 - 9 February 1748 Hynson Wright, Planter, to William Wrench, Planter - consideration 2,000 pounds of tobacco - 26 acres, part of "Guilford," adjoining "Smith's Forrest" - now possessed by Ambrose Wright. Hynson and Sarah his wife (she being first privately examined) acknowledged before William Hopper and Nathaniel Wright.

357. 9 March 1748 Richard Tilghman, Gentleman, to Christopher Phillips, Planter, and Hannah his wife - conveys for the rest of their lives, a tract of land called "Smith's Lott," heretofore conveyed by Chris-Phillips to Richard Tilghman, containing 200 acres - and part of "Winton" and "Winton's Addition" and "Smith's Lott" on Read's Back Creek - adjoining the "Reward." Tilghman reserves the right to cut white oak timber - Christopher and Hannah to keep everything in good repair and not damage the orchard. Acknowledged before Robert Lloyd and Jonathon Nicols, Justices of the Peace.

358. 9 March 1748 Joseph Earle and Elizabeth his wife, to Thomas Wilkinson - consideration 1,500 pounds of tobacco - 175 acres, "Hazard," adjoining "Sawyer's Forrest" and another piece of land called "Burton Upon Wallacy," near the head of Wallacy Creek and adjoining land laid out for Henry Coursey; Samuel Wright, and "Coursey's Range," containing 175 acres. Joseph and Elizabeth (she being first privately examined) acknowledged before William Hopper and Nathaniel Wright.

358. 13 March 1748 John Downes, Planter, to Hynson Downes, Planter - consideration five shillings - 150 acres of land called "Shore-ditch," to revert to John if Hynson should die without lawful issue. Acknowledged before Robert Lloyd and Nathan Wright. Alienation fine paid to Richard Tilghman, six shillings sterling.

359. 13 March 1748 John Downes, Planter, to John Downes, his son - consideration five shillings - 150 acres called "Downeses Chance." To revert to the donor if John dies without lawful issue. Acknowledged before Robert Lloyd and Nathan Wright. Alienation fine, six shillings sterling.

360. 13 March 1748 John Downes, Planter, to James Downes, Planter - consideration five shillings - 100 acres, "Noble's Range" and part of "Arcadia" - on Williams' Branch and adjoining "Shoreditch." Acknowledged before Robert Lloyd and Nathan Wright. Alienation fine, four shillings sterling.

361. 23 September 1748 - 13 March 1748 James Silvester, Sr., Planter, to his son, James Silvester - a gift of 80 acres on Tuckahoe Creek, called (pt.) "Bear Garden." Acknowledged before Edward Tilghman and William Hopper. Alienation fine, three shillings, two pence sterling.

361. 14 December 1748 - 13 March 1748 Richard Porter, Surgin (sic!), to James Ware of Kent County (Md.), Blacksmith - leases 22 acres, part of "Churnell's Neck," with all buildings, for a term of seven years. To include pasturage for one horse, mare or gelding and liberty to cut hay sufficient for his use - twenty acres on the road leading from Collins' Mill to Kings Town and two acres on the west side of the road adjoining a house formerly built for a schoolhouse. Acknowledged before James Brown and Richard Gould.

362. 4 March 1748 - 13 March 1748 Thomas Powel, Planter, and Mary his wife, to Thomas Walker - consideration 2,000 pounds of tobacco - 56 acres called "Tom's Adventure," on Lizenby's Drain. Thomas and Mary (she being first privately examined out of his hearing) acknowledged before James Brown and Humphrey Wells, Jr. Alienation fine, two shillings, three pence sterling.

363. 20 March 1748 - 28 March 1749 Daniel Newnam of Kent County on Delaway, and Elizabeth Newnam, his daughter and daughter of Rachel Newnam, the daughter and devisee of John Hackett, to John Browne, Planter - consideration 2,000 pounds of tobacco - one-third of 100 acres called "Hambleton's Hermitage," bought of William Hambleton of Talbot County and Margaret his wife, 12 February 1701 and devised by John Hackett to his three daughters, Rachell, Hannah and Elizabeth Hackett. Acknowledged before James Brown and Humphrey Wells, Jr. Alienation fine, eight pence sterling.

364. 28 March 1749 Valuation of the land of Margaret Coleman, Josiah Coleman of Talbot County, her guardian. On 27 September, Richard

364. Gould and Thomas Hackett entered upon the land called "Royston" and found one old loged dwelling house, 20 by 15 feet, covered with clapboards; 16 small apple trees and 4 peach trees; containing 33 1/3 acres. Twenty acres is cleared and under very poor fence. We allow one acre to be cleared yearly; the annual rent, 300 pounds of tobacco.

365. 25 March 1749 - 28 March 1749 Isaac Wheeler, Wheelwright, in consideration that Isaac Merrick and Edward Everitt do pay for me to Jeremiah Nicols of Talbot County, Merchant, the sum of 904 pounds of tobacco in cask on 10 November next - do set over one gray mare, one mare colt, one gray horse, one large pyed cow, nine head of hogs and one plow with all the other goods remaining in my dwelling house, per inventory. Wit: Jeremiah Nicols, John Merrick. Acknowledged before Jonathon Nicols.

366. 4 January 1748 - 28 March 1749 Joseph Sudler, Justice of the Peace, appointed Samuel Blunt and John Stevens to view and value the property of Elisha Brown, a minor; his guardian, Nathan Samuel Turbutt Wright - one-fourth part of 170 acres, part of "Cummins' Freehold," "Merson's Freehold" and "Goldhawk's Enlargement," with improvements - being one old dwelling house with two brick gable ends; one old kitchen with brick chimney; one old milk house; one hen house; one small old logg'd house; one 40 feet tobacco house, ruff (sic!) work, all very much out of repair; one small new corn house; one indifferent orchard; a large quantity of indifferent fencing. The annual value, 200 pounds of tobacco clear of quitrents and necessary repairs - the guardian permitted to get timber for repairs and to clear any of the land except for tobacco beds.

366. 9 January 1748 - 29 March 1749 John Collins and William Austin, appointed by Nathan Wright, Justice of the Peace, to make an estimate of the yearly value of lot #37, one acre in Ogletown; the right of Elisha Brown, a minor, his guardian Nathan Samuel Turbutt Wright; did enter upon the land and found one dwelling house, 24 by 16 feet, whole framed, covered with boards - the value one shilling clear of quitrents and necessary repairs.

366. 29 March 1749 Anthony Roe, Planter, to Thomas Roe, Jr. - consideration 5,000 pounds of tobacco and ₤13 current money - three featherbeds and furniture; two horses and one mare colt; six small cattle; eight sheep; one chest of drawers. A mortgage due in three months. Wit: Humphrey Wells, Jr., Henry Coursey. Acknowledged before Humphrey Wells, Jr.

367. 29 November 1748 - 31 March 1749 Reuben Taylor, Planter, to John Tillotson, Gentleman - consideration 8,000 pounds of tobacco - 100 acres, part of "Arcadia," which his father Samuel Taylor devised to him - adjoining a part sold to Solomon Wright. Reuben and Ann his wife (she being first privately examined) acknowledged before William Hopper and Nathan Wright. Alienation fine, four shillings, sterling paid to Richard Tilghman.

368. 30 November 1748 - 31 March 1749 Phillip Connor, Planter, to Charles Connor, Planter - leases 205 acres, part of "Woodyard Thicket," on Kent Island - for a term of twenty years, paying yearly the sum of 2,000 pounds of tobacco; the quitrents and maintaining the said Phillip Connor in Charles' house. Wit: Thomas Barnes, Nathaniel Connor. Acknowledged before William Rogers, Justice of the Provincial Court.

369. 7 March 1748 - 31 March 1749 Henry Poor, Planter, to Mary, wife of John Allen Weddell - consideration 4,400 pounds of tobacco and forty shillings sterling - 100 acres called "Comegys' Hazard" - adjoining the "Lott," on the east side of Long Marsh near the head of Chicken's Marsh. Acknowledged before James Brown and Humphrey Wells, Jr. Alienation fine, four shillings sterling, paid to Richard Tilghman.

370. 31 March 1749 - 1 April 1749 Robert Turner, Planter, to Jonathon Nicols and Sharpless Cooper - consideration 1,400 pounds of tobacco- mortgages six head of cattle for a term of six months. Wit: Andrew Mills. Acknowledged before William Hopper, Jr.

370. 21 January 1745 - 30 April 1749 Edward Alford of Dorchester County, Planter, and Neomey his wife, to Thomas Selvester - consideration 15,000 pounds of tobacco - part of "Selvester's Addition" on the east side of Tuckahoe Creek - bequeathed by Edward Cary of Talbot County, deceased, to his daughter, Neomey Cary. Wit: Thomas Keld, John Russum.

371. 17 April 1749 Abraham Boon and Margaret Banning to James and John Tolson - consideration ₤82 current money - 380 acres called "Partnership," on Plain Branch of Choptank River in Tuckahoe Neck. Abraham and Rebecca his wife (she being first privately examined) acknowledged before Joseph Sudler and Jonathon Nicols. Alienation fine, fifteen shillings, five pence sterling.

372. 19 April 1749 William Coursey and John Walters appointed and sworn by Edward Tilghman, Justice of the Peace, to view and value 200 acres of land, part of "Trustram" - the right of Joseph Thomas, a minor, Edmond Thomas, Sr. his guardian - on 24 December 1748 entered upon the land and found one brick dwelling house, 36 by 18 feet, covered with pine shingles about five years ago; one room below, tiled floor, one room below, plank floor; two rooms above with plank floors. Some of the arches above the doors and windows atumbling out; one tobacco house, 40 by 22 feet with 10 foot pitch, wants covering and new sills immediately and with boards, and doors repaired; one kitchen, 20 by 16 feet with brick chimney and eight foot shed, both covered about four years ago with featheredged oak shingles, wants new sills and the gable end wants repairing; a shed between the kitchen and dwelling house, 16 by 8 feet, covered with featheredged oak shingles about four years ago; a logged quarter, 16 by 12 feet, covered with boards, in pretty good repair; meat house, 12 by 10 feet, covered with boards, wants new sills and cover and with boards repaired; one corne house, 16 by 8 feet, covered with boards,

372. in pretty good repair; one corne house, 8 by 4½ feet, in good repair; one brick shed, 30 by 12 feet, almost down and not worth repairing; an apple orchard of about 160 trees, planted about ten years ago, with good fence; a small cherry walk, the trees but small. The fencing on the plantation in pretty good repair. Annual value, 600 pounds of tobacco clear of quitrents and repairs. The guardian not to clear more land or cut timber except for tobacco hogsheads and necessary repairs, tobacco beds and firewood. 28 December 1748.

373. 28 April 1749 - 4 May 1749 John Davis, Jr., Planter, to John Bracco - consideration ₤12.10.0 paper currency - one negro boy slave named "Mark" - a mortgage due on or before 28 October next. Wit: John Ewing, John Nabb, Jr. Acknowledged before Richard Tilghman, Justice of the Provinical Court.

374. 19 April 1749 - 7 May 1749 Jacob Boon, Planter, to Samuel and William Cook, sons and devisees of James Cook, deceased - releases a mortgage on "Camperson's Choice," made in 1740. Acknowledged before Edward Tilghman and Jonathon Nicols.

374. 6 May 1749 - 1 June 1749 Nathaniel Cleave to Thomas Bailey, Jr. - consideration ₤10 current, 100 bushels of wheat and 15,000 pounds of tobacco - 187 acres, part of "Todley," on the northeast branch of Corsica Creek. Nathaniel and Catherine his wife (she being first privately examined) acknowledged before William Hopper and Nathan Wright. Alienation fine, seven shillings, six pence sterling, paid to Richard Tilghman.

375. 29 May 1749 - 8 June 1749 John Rowe, Planter, to Samuel Rowe, his brother - part of "Tully's Addition," adjoining "Oakenthorp" - to include two tobacco houses, on the part my father lately dwelled on. Acknowledged before James Brown and Nathan Wright. Alienation fine, three shillings sterling.

376. 15 April 1749 - 15 June 1749 Jacob Wootters, Planter, Thomas and Abraham Jump, Planters, to each other - an agreement. Wootters to give the Jump brothers one-half of a grist water mill now a-building on Piney Branch running through "Cow Range" belonging to Jacob Wootters. Thomas and Abraham agree to help with the building of the mill and to pay one-half of the expenses. Wit: John Lumley, James Viney, Margaret Banning.

377. 27 June 1749 James Lloyd, Commander of the ship, "Crichton," at anchor in Chester River in Maryland, bound from thence for London, will take tobacco on board at the rate of ₤7 per tonn freight; 200 hogsheads consigned to Mr. William Anderson, Merchant, in London, the remainder to Mr. James Buchanon, Merchant.

377. 6 June 1749 - 27 June 1749 Jonathon Jolley, in consideration of the sum of ₤5 and the love I bear to my daughter, Anna Jolley, Jr. - after my decease and that of my wife, Anna Jolley, Sr. - convey 50 acres of land called "Andover" on Andover Branch; also 50 acres -

377. "Nicholson's Adventure," lying between the head of Andover and Unicorn Branches; also 57 acres, part of "Burton," adjoining, near the head of Andover Branch. Acknowledged before James Brown and Nathan Wright. Alienation fine, five shillings, 10 pence, half penny sterling, paid to Richard Tilghman.

378. 26 April 1749 - 27 June 1749 Samuel Massey of Chester Town in Kent County (Md.), Merchant, to Daniel Surrell, Merchant - consideration ₤15 current money - Lot Nine in Kings Town, bounded on one side by Front Street, the other by King Street and on the opposite sides by Lots Eight and Sixteen; Lot Twenty, bound by Queen Street, Baltemore Street and Lots Twenty-one and Twenty-nine; also Lot Twenty-three, bound by Chestnut and Queen Streets and by Lots Twenty-two and Twenty-six. Wit: Henry Hooper, Robert Jenckins Henry. Samuel and Sarah his wife (she being first privately examined) acknowledged before Henry Hooper, Justice of the Provincial Court. Alienation fine, two shillings, farthing, sterling.

379. 6 June 1749 - 27 June 1749 Richard Ponder, son of James Ponder, Labourer, to Solomon Seney, Planter - consideration ₤45 paper currency - 75 acres, part of "Clouds' Adventure," on the Cabbin Branch. Acknowledged before James Brown and Nathan Wright. Alienation fine, three shillings, sterling.

380. 26 January 1748 - 29 June 1749 Nathan Samuel Turbutt Wright and Thomas Wright, executors of Thomas Hynson Wright, to William Campbell - according to the will, written 11 September 1747, charging his executors to dispose of his land to pay his debts - in consideration of 18,000 pounds of tobacco and ₤20 current - 330 acres called "Providence," lying between "Partnership," "Royston" and "Shepherd's Fortune." Acknowledged before Robert Lloyd and William Hopper, Jr. Alienation fine, fifteen shillings, two pence, half penny sterling.

381. 25 July 1749 Joseph Hunter, Planter, to William Banckes, Merchant - consideration 2,500 pounds of tobacco - 100 acres, "Hunter's Chance" on an arm of Dickinson's Branch. Joseph and Mary his wife (she being first privately examined) acknowledged before William Hopper, Jr. and Nathan Wright. Alienation fine, four shillings, sterling.

382. 27 July 1749 - 28 July 1749 Abraham Boon to Joseph Tolson - consideration 2,000 pounds of tobacco and ₤9.13.0 sterling - 123 acres, "Tolson's Desire" - lying on the east side of Tuckahoe Creek Branch in a neck called Tuckahoe on the head of the Cow Maide Branch. Abraham and Rebeckah his wife (she being first privately examined) acknowledged before William Hopper, Jr. and Nathan Wright. Alienation fine, seven shillings, nine pence sterling.

383. 14 August 1749 - 27 August 1749 Benjamin Whittington and James Reid, appointed and sworn before James Brown to view and value the land and plantation called "The Laviells" belonging to Margaret Collins, an orphan, now in possession of Robert Sartain, her guardian - entered and found one log'd dwelling house, 16 by 12 feet, covered

383. with ruff clabboards; one house, 12 by 10, covered with ruff clabboards; one log corn house, 16 by 18 feet; two old 20-feet log'd tobacco houses, 20 feet wide, very much out of repair; nine old apell (sic!) trees; 10 old pech (sic!) trees; in the tract about 160 acres and about 80 acres cleared. The guardian allowed one acre of land per year for repairs; the annual value, 700 pounds of tobacco.

383. 12 April 1740 - 22 August 1749 James Reid and Benjamin Whittington, appointed and sworn by James Brown to view and value "Ry Hall," belonging to George Ayers, an orphan, now possessed by Jacob Dodd, his guardian - entered upon the land and found one dwelling house, 30 by 18 feet with two brick chimneys and plank floors, shingled with featheredged shingles, much out of repair; one house, 20 by 12 feet, with featheredged shingles and brick chimney and an oven in the chimney, covered with featheredged shingles; one 5 by 8 feet milk house, covered with featheredged shingles, much out of repair; one corn house, 20 feet long; one tobacco house, 30 feet long, covered with ruff clabboards; 27 apple trees, 6 cherry trees; about 120 acres, almost all cleared in very poor repair. Jacob Dodd to clear one acre for repairs. Annual value, 350 pounds of tobacco yearly.

384. 22 August 1749 John Scotten to Thomas Burroughs, now of Kent County (Md.) - consideration £30 - 55 acres of land called "Scotten's Inclosure." Scotten's receipt to Burroughs witnessed by John Chaires. Acknowledged before James Brown and Humphrey Wells, Jr. Alienation fine, two shillings, two pence sterling, paid to Richard Tilghman.

385. 16 August 1749 - 22 August 1749 Richard Porter, Jr., Chyrurgeon, to Edward Tilghman, Gentleman - consideration £60.5.3 sterling money of Great Britain and £190.14.0 paper currency of Maryland - 200 acres, all of "Churnell's Neck," heretofore in Talbot County but now in Queen Anne County in a fork of the eastern branch of Chester River - adjoining the Beaverdamb - and part of "Annthorpe," originally granted to William Hemsley and sold to Richard Porter by John Hollingsworth, 11 July 1743 - adjoining the part sold to William Campbell - also 60 acres, part of "Annthorpe," sold to Richard Porter by Nicholas Broadway, 14 September 1748 - at Wills Hole - adjoining "Churnell's Neck" and "Whitehall" - containing in the whole 203 acres. This mortgage due on or before 20 December 1752. Wit: Richard Tilghman and John Porter. Acknowledged before Richard Tilghman, Justice of the Provincial Court, Sarah, wife of Richard Porter having been first privately examined out of his hearing.

387. 24 August 1749 Robert Sumpter, Planter, and Sarah his wife, to Jeremiah Jadwin - in consideration of certain debts to be paid for him - conveys one cow; two heifers; one horse and mair (sic!); one featherbed, bedsted, cord and blue rugg, blanket and two sheets; one featherbed, bolster and cord; one pide rugg; two blankets and two pillows; one frying pan; six chaires; one plow shear and colter; five sheep; fourteen hoggs - all on my plantation. Robert and Sarah (she being first privately examined) acknowledged before James Brown and Nathan Wright.

389. 29 March 1749 - 25 August 1749 Humphrey Wells to Elizabeth and Mary Swift, his granddaughters - a gift of love and affection - 100 acres, "Crump's Advice," lying in the Forrest of Choptank on the west side of the road from Chester to the head of Choptank River. Witnessed by James Brown and Benjamin Roberts. Acknowledged before James Brown and Humphrey Wells, Jr. Alienation fine, four shillings sterling, paid to Richard Tilghman.

390. 19 August 1749 - 26 August 1749 Anthony Roe, Planter, and Jane his wife, to Benjamin Roberts, Planter - consideration ₤30 current and 3,000 pounds of tobacco - 100 acres, part of "Sawyear's Range" - on the south side of Read Lion Branch (sic!). Anthony and Jane (she being first privately examined) acknowledged before James Brown and Humphrey Wells, Jr. Alienation fine, four shillings, sterling.

392. 26 August 1749 - 31 August 1749 Matthew Dockery, Gentleman, and Sarah his wife, to Arthur Emory, Sr., Planter - consideration ₤50 sterling and ₤80 paper currency - 100 acres called "Moore's Hope" on Chester Mill Branch about one mile above Stephen Rich's plantation; 208 acres, part of "Moore's Hope Addition." Matthew and Sarah (she being first privately examined) acknowledged before William Hopper, Jr. Alienation fine, twelve shillings, four pence sterling.

393. 15 August 1749 - 31 August 1749 William Driskell, Carpenter, to Thomas Powell of Talbot County - consideration 866 pounds of tobacco - one gray gelding named "Buck," about eight years old - the same bought of Thomas Clark of Talbot County. Wit: Edward Nedels, Edward Nedels, Jr.

393. 26 September 1749 - 28 September 1749 Richard Bennett to Joseph All, son of William All - consideration ₤50 current money paid by William All, the father of James - 100 acres, part of "Oakenthorp," patented to Richard Bennett for 1,000 acres - lying in Tully's Neck in the branches of Tuckahoe Creek - adjoining Thomas Hyndsley. Wit: Edward Neale, Jo. Loockerman, Jr. Acknowledged before Richard Tilghman, Justice of the Provincial Court. Alienation fine, four shillings, sterling.

394. 11 November 1749 - 28 November 1749 Charles Talbot of Lunenburgh County, Colony of Virginia, Planter, to Thomas Sands, Planter - consideration ₤55 current money - 119 acres called "Lanchester," by the Green Swamp, adjoining Thomas Bostock's land, "Northumberland." Acknowledged before William Hopper, Jr. and Nathan Wright. Alienation fine, four shillings, nine pence, half penny sterling.

395. 29 November 1749 William Newnam, Planter, to Nathaniel Newnam - in consideration of a negro girl named "Kate" - 93 acres, part of land called "Shaver," lying on the west side of the Unicorn Branch - originally surveyed for Francis Shippard for 200 acres and sold to Francis Mitchell about 21 June 1687; acknowledged and recorded in Talbot County and by Robert Taylor and Frances his wife, conveyed to Richard Bennett, the deed acknowledged and recorded in Queen Anne County.

395. and by Richard Bennett to William Newman, acknowledged and recorded in Queen Anne County. Wit: Philemon Hemsley, John Emory. Acknowledged in Court at Queens Town before James Brown and Associates. Alienation fine, three shillings, nine pence sterling, paid to Richard Tilghman.

397. 29 November 1749 - 30 November 1749 William Hopper, Gentleman, to Caleb Esgate, Planter - lease of part of "Stepney," where he now dwells on Red Lyon Branch - term, ten years; annual rent, 1,000 pounds of tobacco. Wit: Robert Hardcastle, N. Wright. Acknowledged before N. Wright and John Seegar, Justices of the Peace.

397. 30 November 1749 William Sedgley, Commander of the ship, "Chester," lying at Chester Town in Chester River, will take tobacco on freight at ₤7 per tonn, consigned to Messrs. Sedgley and Cheston, Merchants in Bristol.

398. 2 December 1749 Philemon Hemsley to his sister, Anna Maria Hemsley - a gift of love - the tract of land called "Hardestfendoff." Acknowledged before Nathan WRight and John Downes, Justices of the Peace.

398. 2 December 1749 Philemon Hemsley to his sister, Mary Hemsley - a gift of love - two tracts of land called "Toutonfield's Addition" and "Hemsley's Discovery." Acknowledged before Nathan Wright and John Downes.

399. 9 December 1749 Richard Tilghman, Esquire, to Michael Earle of Cecil County, Gentleman - recovery of 270 acres called "Emory's Fortune Addition," and part of "Partnership," 175 acres, contiguous. Acknowledged before Nathan Wright and John Downes. [Reference made to a Writ of Entry previously made.]

399. 23 December 1749 Nathan Samuel Turbutt Wright, Gentleman, and heir at law of Thomas Hynson Wright; and Thomas Wright, his brother, to James Ringgold of Eastern Neck in Kent County (Md.), Gentleman - consideration ₤725 current money - 800 acres of land, part of "Coursey's Point alias Smith's Mistake," "Bishop's Addition," "Bishop's Outlett" and "Brampton's Addition" - where William Bishop lately lived; also where John Chaires and James Stinson now live - lying on Coursica Creek and adjoining the lands of William Hopper, Ernault Hawkins, Richard Bennett, Christopher Cox, Thomas Bailey, Samuel Austin and others. Wit: Richard Tilghman Earle, H. J. Johnson. Nathan Samuel Turbutt Wright and Dorcas his wife (she being first privately examined) and Thomas Wright acknowledged before Richard Tilghman, a Justice of the Provincial Court.

401. 23 December 1749 - 29 December 1749 Joseph Dodd, Planter, and Mary his wife, sole daughter and heir of George Mattershaw, deceased, to John Jackson, Chyrurgeon - consideration 7,500 pounds of tobacco - 40 acres, part of "Jamaica" - on the branches of Coursica Creek. Joseph and Mary (she being first privately examined) acknowledged before William Hopper, Jr. and Nathan Wright. Alienation fine,

401. twenty pence sterling, paid to Richard Tilghman.

402. 17 January 1749 William Dames to the Reverend James Cox - whereas Rev. Cox has paid for me to the Honorable Phillip Thomas, Esquire, the sum of ₤100 paper currency with costs of the suit to be paid to Mr. James Dick; ₤142 sterling with costs, also to Mr. John Wallace & Company; between 7,000 and 8,000 pounds of tobacco and also secured to be paid to the executor of Richard Bennett between ₤90 and ₤100 sterling with interest; also 1,500 pounds of tobacco paid the Sheriff of Queen Anne County - in consideration of the premises and to secure to James Cox the repayment, convey the following slaves: one negro man, "Harry" and his wife, "Venus," their three children, i.e. "Dorothy," "Martha" and "William;" one negro man, "Peter," his wife "Priscilla" and their two children; one negro woman, "Rachel;" one negro girl, "Rachel;" seven head of horses, mares and colts; ten head of horned cattle, young and old; twenty-five head of sheep; a chaise and harness; all the grain, plantation tools, household furniture, pieces of plate and all effects that belong to me, now on the plantation and in the actual possession of James Cox - a chattel mortgage due in six months. Acknowledged before Richard Tilghman, Justice of the Provincial Court.

403. 5 February 1749 - 12 February 1749 John Davis, Jr., Planter, to Christopher Cox Routh, Planter - consideration ₤8 current money of Maryland, of which to me paid the sum of ₤6.10.10 current - one cow; two steers, two years old; two stears, one year old (marks given). Wit: Thomas Yoe, William Bennett. Acknowledged before William Hopper.

404. 14 February 1749 - 15 February 1749 John Davis, Jr. to John Bracco - in consideration of ₤3 paper and two pieces of eight - a negro boy named "Jamey;" likewise a mortgage on a negro boy named "Mark," executed 28th day April last, the bond received and release of the mortgage. Wit: Ambrose Wright, Thomas Obryon. Acknowledged before Nathan Wright.

404. 12 February 1749/50 - 15 February 1749 John Davis, Jr., Planter, to Edward Clayton - consideration ₤40 current money and 2,500 pounds of tobacco - a negro woman named "Judah" and a negro boy named "Nathan." Acknowledged before William Hopper.

404. 16 FEbruary 1749 John Davis, son of Thomas Davis, deceased, to Thomas Obryon, his security for sundry sums - do, in consideration of 3,500 pounds of tobacco, sell one negro boy named "Mark," about six years old. Acknowledged before Richard Tilghman, Justice of the Provincial Court.

405. 8 December 1749 - 16 February 1749 Edward Tobin, Planter, to William Coursey, Gentleman - in consideration of ₤14 current money - a moiety of 50 acres of "Smeath," formerly in Talbot County, now in Queen Anne - which Robert Walters of Talbot County, Planter, in a deed made 3 June 1697, conveyed to John Etherington, Planter, who

405. paid 6,000 pounds of tobacco for the land - lying on the east side of Morgan's Creek, a branch of Wye River. Acknowledged before John Downes, Jr. and John Downes. Alienation fine, six pence sterling, paid to Richard Tilghman.

406. 24 February 1749 - 8 March 1749 John Davis, Jr. in consideration of 654 pounds of tobacco to be paid to Capt. Edward Tilghman by Christopher Cross Routh, as security for 16 shillings and 4 pence sterling, a debt due Christopher Cross Routh from John Davis, Jr. - conveys three cows and three yearlings. Acknowledged before Nathan Wright.

407. 8 March 1749/50 John Davis, Jr. to William Simmonds of Kent County (Md.), in consideration of ₤5.2.0 current money of Maryland - one small mare colt under one year old and one old chest. Acknowledged before William Hopper.

407. 24 November 1749 - 8 March 1749 Thomas Nicholson and Mary his wife, to Thomas Jackson - consideration 3,500 pounds of tobacco - 50 acres called "Nicholson's Chance" - lying on Devinishes Branch, out of the Unicorn Branch. Acknowledged before James Brown and William Hopper. Alienation fine, two shillings sterling, paid to Richard Tilghman.

408. 16 February 1749 - 8 March 1749 John Davis, Jr., son and heir of Thomas Davis, to Richard Tilghman, Gentleman - 70 acres, part of "Content," near the dwelling plantation of John Davis; 232 acres, part of "Content;" 50 acres called "Beaver Dams;" 50 acres called "Hollow Flat" - mortgaged 9 July 1745 by Thomas Davis in consideration of the sum of ₤138.8.0 current money paid by Richard Tilghman; two parts of "Content," whereon Thomas Davis did dwell; all of "Beaver Dams," purchased of Edward Wright; also all of "Hollow Flat," purchased of Thomas Bostock - the mortgage due before 10 November and not yet paid. Acknowledged before William Hopper and Nathan Wright.

410. 12 March 1749 - 27 March 1750 Walter Dulany of Annarundel County and Mary his wife, to Christopher Cox, Gentleman - consideration ₤200 sterling money of Great Britain and ₤20 Maryland currency - a moiety of "Partnership," formerly surveyed for William Tilghman and Francis Shepard in joint tenancy - containing 1,000 acres, at the head of Royston's Creek adjoining "Ward Park," now in possession of William Carmichall - the moiety, 500 acres. Cox's receipt witnessed by Thomas Hyde and Jonas Green. Acknowledged before John Brice, a Justice of the Provincial Court, Mary Dulany examined out of hearing of her husband. Alienation fine, twenty shillings sterling.

412. __ Nove. 1749 - 28 March 1750 Sarah Hollyday, Widow, to her son, Henry Hollyday - a gift of love and affection - negro slaves, vizt: "Great Jack," his wife "Bell" and her three children, "Hannah," "Wally" and "Abel;" "Peter," "Felix," "Boy Jack," "Gilderoy," "Harry,"

412. "Peggy" and her two children, "Isaac" and "Charles;" eight head of horses; twenty black cattle; thirty head of sheep. Wit: James Hollyday.

412. 11 December 1749 - 28 March 1750 William Dames, Merchant, to Peter Maxwell, Joyner - consideration twenty shillings current money - lease of his lot, Number Three in Kings Town - lately purchased of John Hollingsworth and where he lately dwelt - term of one year. Wit: Thomas Ringgold, James Moore, Jr.

413. 12 December 1749 - 28 March 1750 William Dames, Merchant, to Peter Maxwell, Joyner - consideration ₤65 current money of Maryland - sells lot Number Three in Kings Town. Wit: Thomas Ringgold, James Moore, Jr. Alienation fine, three farthings sterling, paid to Richard Tilghman.

413. 29 March 1750 Charles Downes, guardian of Charles Clayton, a minor, petitioned for an evaluation of the orphan's estate. John Seegar, Justice of the Peace, appointed Joseph Elliott and William Newnam, 15 February 1749, to view and value 108 acres of land called "Mt. Molock." They entered and found two old logged dwelling houses of round loggs, fifteen feet in length, much out of repair; two old tobacco houses, 30 feet in length, much out of repair; eighty-four apple trees and a few old peach trees; fifty acres cultivated, under very poor fence. Annual value, 400 pounds of tobacco exclusive of quitrents; the guardian to get timber for repairs and to clear one and one-half acres yearly.

414. 29 March 1750 Edward Tilghman, Gentleman, to Andrew Carrer, Planter - part of "Resurvey of Forlorn Hope Rectified" - for and during the natural life of the said Andrew, the rent, 1,000 pounds of tobacco in hogsheads paid by 10 December yearly. Andrew agreed to plant 100 cattling apple trees, fifty feet asunder as soon as may be, the site to be selected by Tilghman and secured by good fence and keep trimmed and pruned. Acknowledged before Nathan Wright and John Downs, Jr.

415. 29 March 1750 John Scotten, Planter, to Edward Tilghman - consideration ₤11.13.4 - fifty acres near John's dwelling plantation called "Scotten's Folley" - lying in the fork of the main branch of Chestter River. Acknowledged before Nathan Wright and John Downs, Jr. Alienation fine, five shillings sterling, paid to Richard Tilghman.

416. 30 January 1749 - 29 March 1750 William Goldsborough of Talbot County, Gentleman; James Troth, Planter, and James Tilghman of Talbot County, Gentleman - an indenture tripartite regarding a Writ of Entry executed in May 1748 against James Tilghman - Goldsborough and Troth release and quitclaim to Tilghman their claim to three hundred acres of land in Queen Anne County called "Cole Banks" and one hundred acres called "Cole Banks Addition." Acknowledged before Thomas Bozman and Jeremiah Nicols, Justices of the Peace for Talbot County - certified by John Leeds, Clerk.

417. 28 December 1749 - 5 April 1750 Thomas Lee, Planter, to Philemon Thomas, Planter - consideration ₤20 current money - 33 acres, part of "Lee's Chance," lying in the fork of the main branch of Tuckahoe Creek. Acknowledged before Nathan Wright and N. Wright. Alienation fine, one shilling, four pence sterling, paid to Richard Tilghman.

418. 6 April 1750 This indenture of three parts, Nathan Wright and Mary his wife of the one; William Bishop, Planter of the second; and Edward Tilghman, Gentleman, of the third. For the purpose of docking and barring of all estate tail, Nathan and Mary convey to Bishop parts of "Long Neck" and "Coursey Upon Wye," devised to Mary Wright by her father, Major William Turbutt, deceased - beginning at the lower landing of Edward Tilghman (formerly the lower landing of Major Turbutt), near the dwelling house of Edward Tilghman (formerly Major Turbutt's), on or near the road leading from Tilghman's dwelling plantation to Queens Town - adjoining Maurice Shehawn's plantation, Carroll's East Branch and Carroll's Cove of Wye River - containing 324 acres and one messuage thereon. William Bishop, before the end of the April term of court to permit Edward Tilghman to sue for a Writ of Entry to recover the land. Wit: Richard Tilghman, William Hopper, John Jackson. Acknowledged by all parties (Mary, wife of Nathan Wright being first privately examined) before Richard Tilghman, Justice of the Provincial Court. Alienation fine, thirteen shillings sterling.

419. 27 February 1749 - 6 April 1750 Richard Porter of Talbot County, Chyrurgeon, and Alice his wife, to Matthew Tilghman, Gentleman - consideration ₤136.5.0 current money - one-half of a tract of land lying on the easternmost branch of Andover Branch called "Timber Neck," containing 250 acres; and one-half of a tract called "Negligence," containing 24½ acres, formerly the estate of John Evans late of Kent County (Md.), deceased, the only uncle of the said Alice, now wife of Richard Porter. Richard and Alice (she being first privately examined) acknowledged before Robert Goldsborough and Jacob Hindman, certified by John Leeds, Clerk of the Talbot County Court. Alienation fine, eleven shillings sterling.

421. 7 April 1750 Richard Tilghman, Gentleman, to John Davis, Gentleman - consideration ₤60 current - 70 acres called "Content," commonly called the Swamp. Richard and Susanna his wife (she being first privately examined) acknowledged before William Hopper and Nathan Wright. Alienation fine, two shillings, ten pence sterling.

422. 12 April 1750 Philemon Hemsley to John Downes, Planter - consideration 1,000 pounds of tobacco - quitclaim to 200 acres called "Noble's Range," now in the possession of John Davis. Wit: Richard Tilghman, Henry Johnson. Acknowledged before Richard Tilghman.

422. 14 April 1750 Robert Fowler, Planter, to Richard Tilghman, Gentleman - reference to a mortgage made 2 July 1743 amounting to ₤31.10.0 on 150 acres of land called (pt.) "Shrewsbury" whereon Robert Fowler then dwelt, he to pay before 10 November 1747 the sum borrowed

422. with legal interest for the redemption, which has not been paid. The land conveyed is the easternmost half of "Shrewsbury." Robert Fowler and Mary his wife (she being first privately examined out of his hearing) acknowledged before William Hopper and Nathan Wright.

423. 13 April 1750 - 16 April 1750 Philemon Hemsley, Gentleman, to William Campbell - consideration ₤40 sterling and 6,500 pounds of tobacco - 66 acres, part of "Lloyd's Meadows" - adjoining "Carpenter's Square" - on Thomases Branch. Wit: James Lloyd, Robert Lloyd. Acknowledged before Richard Tilghman, Justice of the Provincial Court. Alienation fine, two shillings sterling.

424. 19 April 1750 Philemon Hemsley to John Downes - consideration 1,000 pounds of tobacco - quitclaim to 142 acres, part of "Noble's Range," adjoining Young's land and a parcel of land sold by Henry Costin to John Jones. Acknowledged before William Hopper and N. Wright.

425. 19 April 1750 Philemon Hemsley to Henry Jones, Planter - consideration 1,000 pounds of tobacco - 58 acres, part of "Noble's Range," now in possession of Henry Jones. Acknowledged before William Hopper and N. Wright.

425. 2 April 1750 - 19 April 1750 Philemon Hemsley, Gentleman, to his sisters, Anna Maria and Mary Hemsley - a gift of love and affection - 462 acres, one-half of "Towton Fields" - lying within the division made between my father and Samuel Broadway; one-half to each. Acknowledged before Nathan Wright and John Downes, Jr.

426. 19 April 1750 Richard Tilghman, Gentleman, to Robert Fowler and Mary his wife - lease of one-half of his late purchase of Fowler, part of "Shrewsbury," lying on the side next to the widow Merriday's, for and during their natural lives - the rent, 500 pounds of tobacco per annum. Fowler to plant and orchard of fifty apple trees and fence in; Tilghman to provide nails for a dwelling house, 20 by 16 feet and a tobacco house, 30 by 22 feet and pay towards the building thereof, 1,800 pounds of tobacco. Wit: Nathan Wright, Richard Tilghman Earle. Acknowledged before William Hopper and N. Wright.

427. 24 May 1750 Benjamin Kirby of the Isle of Kent, Gentleman, to Elizabeth Thompson of Chester Town, Kent County (Md.), Widow - consideration ₤30 current money - 52 acres on the Isle of Kent called "Kirby's Recovery," adjoining "Little Ease" on the west side of Cox'es Creek - patented 20 April 1748. Wit: Emory Sudler, Solomon Wright. Acknowledged before Richard Tilghman, Justice of the Provincial Court. Alienation fine, two shillings, one pence sterling.

427. 1 May 1750 - 24 May 1750 Nathan Samuel Turbutt Wright and Thomas Wright, Gentleman, to James Finley, Wheelwright - consideration 2,700 pounds of tobacco - 27 acres called "Nathan and Thomas' Beginning" - adjoining "Solomon's Friendship" and in the south line of His Lordship's Manor. Acknowledged before James Brown and N. Wright. Alienation fine, one shilling, one pence sterling.

428. 9 February 1749 - 24 May 1750 William Rickerds, Carpenter, to Absalom Sparks - consideration 6,000 pounds of tobacco and ₤15 current money - 100 acres, part of "Folly's Delight" - lying on the south side of Back Creek in Chester River. William and Mary his wife (she being first privately examined out of his hearing) acknowledged before William Hopper and Nathan Wright. Alienation fine, two shillings sterling, paid to Richard Tilghman.

429. 22 July 1750 Joseph Roe, Blacksmith, to Samuel Roe - consideration 10,000 pounds of tobacco - 150 acres, part of "Tully's Addition," which descended to Joseph by the will of his deceased grandfather, John Roe - lying in the fork of the northernmost branch of Tuckahoe Creek. Also 27 acres, all of "Roe's Lane," adjoining "Robinson's Farm;" also part of "Ned's Beginning" and also part of "Sarah's Fancy," all adjoining to "Tully's Addition." Acknowledged before Jonathon Nicols and N. Wright. Alienation fine, six shillings, four pence, half penny sterling.

430. 5 May 1750 - 31 May 1750 Margaret Chaires, Widow, of St. Paul's Parish, to her son John Chaires, Planter - a gift of love - 200 acres of land, a moiety of "Wrenches Farm;" separated from the other part by Rowbottom's Branch - now in her possession and occupation. Acknowledged before William Hopper and Nathan Wright. Alienation fine, eight shillings sterling.

431. 9 June 1750 - 13 June 1750 John Davis, Jr. to Nathan Wright, Jr. - consideration 6,000 pounds of tobacco - part of "Content" - lying on the northernmost branch of Coursica Creek - the residue not mortgaged or sold to Col. Richard Tilghman. John Davis and Esther, his wife (she being first privately examined) acknowledged before William Hopper and Nathan Wright. Alienation fine, nine shillings, five pence.

432. 14 April 1750 - 13 June 1750 John Weeks, Planter, and Mary his wife, to Dowdall Thompson - consideration 2,500 pounds of tobacco - 52½ acres, part of "Mt. Pleasant," on the south side of Chester River. John and Mary (she being first privately examined) acknowledged before James Brown and John Seegar.

433. 16 April 1750 - 26 June 1750 William Spry to Christopher Spry - consideration 900 pounds of tobacco - 11 acres, part of "Friendship," a division made by his father, Francis Spry. Acknowledged before James Brown and John Seegar. Alienation fine, five pence, half penny, sterling.

434. 6 February 1749 - 26 June 1750 Thomas Teat, Planter, and Sarah his wife, to Benjamin Smith, Planter - consideration ₤62 current money - 30 acres, "Mary's Chance," lying on the east side of Becklesses Branch of Chester River - adjoining "Wiatt's Lott." Also 32 acres, "Teat's Desire," lying on a branch of Double Creek and adjoining "Wiatt's Lott." Thomas and Sarah (she being first privately examined) acknowledged before James Brown and Nathan Wright. Alienation

434. fine, seven shillings, seven pence, half penny sterling, paid to Richard Tilghman.

435. 24 May 1750 - 26 June 1750 Benjamin Thomas, Planter, to Philemon Thomas, Planter - consideration ₤150 current money - 60 acres, part of "Hawkins Pharsalia," lying in Tully's Neck in the fork of the main branch of Tuckahoe Creek - left by Trustram Thomas to Benjamin Thomas. Acknowledged before John Downes, Jr. and N. Wright. Alienation fine, two shillings, two pence sterling.

436. 26 June 1750 John Smyth and Charles Conner, lawfully qualified by Joseph Sudler to make a just estimate of the value of the land called "Sillin" on Kent Island, belonging to the heirs of Sarah Price, deceased, entered 20 April 1750 and found one dwelling house, out of repair, 24 by 18 feet, brick gables and plastered above and below, a shed the length of the house, brick chimley, plastered; a brick seller; one small kitchin, brick chimley; an old logg corn house; one middling 40 feet tobacco house; 47 old apple trees, a few peach and cherrie (sic!) trees; the fences in very good repair; on one tenement thereon there is one old logg dwelling house, a good tobacco house; an old logg corn house; one other tenement whereon is an old logg dwelling house. The land worth 1,800 pounds of tobacco per annum, one-third part of the property belongs to Mary Evins, daughter of Sarah Price.

436. 8 June 1750 - 26 June 1750 Thomas Butler to William Clayton - consideration ₤50 current - a negro man named "Peter." Wit: Jonathon Arey, Anne Wright, Philemon Murphy. Acknowledged before Nathan Wright. A bond given to secure payment of Thomas Butler's debts.

437. 3 January 1749 - 29 June 1750 William Dames, Merchant, to Samuel Massey of Chester Town, Merchant - consideration ₤250 current - a tract of land on Chester River near Kings Town called "Chestnut Neck," containing 300 acres - lately bought of John Hamer and Sarah Firth. Wit: Josiah Willson, Thomas Taylor. Acknowledged before George Steuart, Justice of the Provincial Court.

438. 10 July 1750 - 17 July 1750 A deed in four parts between John Hall of the first part; William Hall of the second; Edward Hall of the third and Lawrence Hall of the fourth part. A division of 300 acres of land called "Hogg Harbour," recently patented and granted 9 September 1748. Each to receive 73¼ acres, except for 7 acres of John's part, taken away by an elder survey called "Dancy." Acknowledged before N. Wright and John Downes.

440. 10 July 1750 - 17 July 1750 William Hall to John Hall - consideration ₤20 - 73¼ acres, part of "Hogg Harbour." William Hall and Luisa his wife (she being first privately examined) acknowledged before N. Wright and John Downes. Alienation fine, two shillings, eleven pence sterling.

441. 10 July 1750 - 17 July 1750 Lawrence Hall to Edward Hall - consider-

441. ation ₤20 current money - 73¼ acres, part of "Hogg Harbour." Lawrence Hall and Mary Ann his wife (she being first privately examined out of his hearing) acknowledged before N. Wright and John Downes.

441. 5 May 1750 - 17 July 1750 George Smith and Mary his wife, to Robert Smith, Planter - consideration 4,000 pounds of tobacco - 100 acres, part of "Tom's Fancy Enlarged." (number of acres not specified). George and Mary (she being first privately examined) acknowledged before William Hopper, Jr. and Nathan Wright. Alienation fine, four shillings sterling, paid to Richard Tilghman.

442. 5 June 1750 - 17 July 1750 Arnault Hawkins and Jane his wife, to Charles Raley - consideration ₤29 current money - 90 acres of land on the east side of the Beaver Dam Marsh, called "Hawkins Range." Arnault and Jane (she being first privately examined) acknowledged before Nathan Wright and John Seegar. Alienation fine, four shillings sterling.

443. 2 February 1749 - 17 July 1750 John Baker, Planter, of St. Mary's County, to William Hughlett; Thomas Hughlett, his son and James Genn of the Colony of Virginia, Gentleman - consideration ₤80 in gold or silver currency - 600 acres called "Baker's Plains," lying near the head of Great Choptank River - a warrant granted to John Baker, Innholder, father of the aforesaid John Baker, 17 July 1680 and laid out 6 August of the same year - adjoining "Old Town." James Genn is to have 200 acres at the easternmost part. Acknowledged before Richard Barnhouse and James Biscoe, Justices of the Peace for St. Mary's County; Elizabeth Baker, wife of John, examined before making her acknowledgment. Richard Ward Key, Clerk of St. Mary's County. Alienation fine, one pound, four shillings sterling.

444. 14 May 1750 - 24 July 1750 William Bussels, Cordwinder, and Margaret his mother, to Henry Rochester, Planter - consideration ₤50 Maryland currency - 50 acres called "Philadelphia," lying on the west side of Red Lion Branch - adjoining "Slaughterton." William and his mother, Margaret (she being first privately examined) acknowledged before James Brown and John Seegar. Alienation fine, two shillings sterling paid to Richard Tilghman.

445. 8 May 1750 - 26 July 1750 William Winchester Mason, Planter, to his brother, Solomon Mason - a gift of love and with compliance with the last words of his father - 133 acres, part of "Winchester's Folly Resurveyed," lying on the east side of the main branch of Tuckahoe Creek. Acknowledged before N. Wright and John Downes. Alienation fine, five shillings, four pence sterling.

446. 5 May 1750 - 26 July 1750 William Winchester Mason, Planter, to his brother, Richard Mason - a gift of love and with compliance with the last words of his father - 133 acres, part of "Winchester's Folly Resurveyed," lying on the east side of the main branch of Tuckahoe Creek. Acknowledged before N. Wright and John Downes. Alienation fine, five shillings, four pence sterling.

447. 26 July 1750 George Smith and N. Wright, Jr., qualified by Nathan Wright to make a just estimate of the annual valuation of one-third part of "Upper Deal," the right of Anne Evans; Joseph Evans, her guardian - on 27 April 1750 entered upon the plantation and after consideration thereof, did value the land at 500 pounds of tobacco per annum, clear of quitrents and necessary repairs.

447. 28 July 1749 - 14 May 1750 I, John Elliott with consent, doe part with my wife with her consent and promise not to take anything from her as I give to her and I doe give her a horse, a cow and calf, a bed, a large trunk and part of ye rest of ye household goods and I, his wife, doe promise not to come upon him for anything else. Written on the back: I doe hereby set over my right and title and interest to Abraham Betton. 16 July 1750. Sig: Rachell Elliott. Wit: Thomas Walker.

447. 28 July 1750 Rachell Elliott, Spinster, to Abraham Betton, Jobber - one large black horse, about ten or eleven years old; one cow and one calf; one dozen pewter plates; one-half dozen earthen plates; one large trunk. Wit: Thomas Walker, William Cowman.

448. 2 August 1750 Daniel Knott of Talbot County, Practitioner of Physick and Frances his wife, the daughter and devisee of William Ratcliff of Queen Anne's County, deceased, to Benjamin Whittington, Gentleman - consideration ₤50 current money - 83 acres, one-half of a parcel of land near St. Luke's Church, called "Ratcliff's part of Lloyd's Freshes," devised to Frances by the will of William Ratcliff. Daniel and Frances (she being first privately examined) acknowledged before William Hopper and Nathan Wright. Alienation fine, three farthings, two pence, half penny sterling, paid to Richard Tilghman.

449. 11 August 1750 - 17 August 1750 John Cook of Dorchester County to Thomas Baggs - consideration 4,000 pounds of tobacco - one negro woman named "Daphney." Wit: John Lumley, Thomas Wilkinson. Acknowledged before Nathan Wright.

449. 20 July 1750 - 17 August 1750 Matthew Hawkins, Planter, and Frances his wife, to John Hawkins, Planter - consideration 5,000 pounds of tobacco - 107 acres, part of "Tully's Delight" - lying on the west side of Island Creek (the part willed to Matthew Hawkins by his father, John Hawkins). Acknowledged before William Hopper and Nathan Wright.

449. 20 July 1750 - 21 August 1750 John Hawkins, Planter, and Sarah his wife, to Matthew Hawkins, Planter - consideration 10,000 pounds of tobacco and ₤5 current money of Maryland - 200 acres on the west side of Island Creek, part of "Tully's Delight." John and Sarah (she being first privately examined) acknowledged before William Hopper and Nathan Wright. Alienation fine, four shillings sterling.

450. 24 August 1750 James Salsbury, Planter, to Richard Tilghman, Gentleman - consideration 17,000 pounds of tobacco and ₤28 current money -

450. 187 acres called "Sintra," lying at the mouth of Corsica Creek. James and Frances his wife (she being first privately examined out of his hearing) acknowledged before William Hopper and Nathan Wright.

451. 28 August 1750 Daniel Smith, Planter, to Benjamin Smith, Planter - a division of "Jones' Fancy," willed to Daniel, Benjamin and Casparus Smith by their father, Casparus Smith in his will written 31 July, 1735 (Casparus (Jr.) a minor at the time.) Acknowledged before N. Wright and John Seegar.

452. 7 August 1750 - 29 August 1750 William Young, Planter, to Thomas Lee - consideration ₤51 current - 52 acres, part of "Stratton" - adjoining his brother John Young's, land. William and Elizabeth, his wife (she being first privately examined) acknowledged before Nathan and N. Wright. Alienation fine, two shillings, one pence sterling.

453. 1 September 1750 Certificate of estray: Jeremiah Grasingham brought before me a dark roan mare, a star in her forehead, without a brand; a squat low mare about four years old; the owner proving his property and paying the charges may have her. Certified by John Downes.

453. 18 August 1750 - 1 September 1750 Thomas Stanton, Planter, to John Downes, Jr. - consideration 4,000 pounds of tobacco - 60 acres, part of "Security," lying between the head of the Long Marsh and the Beaverdam Marsh. Acknowledged before William Hopper and Nathan Wright. Alienation fine, two shillings, five pence sterling.

454. 15 September 1750 - 19 September 1750 John Allen Wooddell, Planter, and Mary his wife, to Thomas Carradine - consideration ₤35 current - 100 acres called "Comegys Hazard," adjoining the "Lott" - on the east side of Long Marsh, near the head of Chicken Marsh. John Allen and Mary (she being first privately examined) acknowledged before William Hopper and Thomas Hammond.

455. 29 August 1750 - 20 September 1750 John Ayler, Taylor, to William Banckes, Merchant - consideration ₤40 - 97 acres called "Ayler's Outlet" - on the east side of the mainbranch of Tuckahoe Creek, near Charles Bradley's dwelling house. Acknowledged before N. Wright and William Hopper.

456. 29 August 1750 - 20 September 1750 Edward Everett to William Banckes, Merchant - consideration 1,800 pounds of tobacco - 50 acres called "James' Park" - adjoining "Hunter's Hope." Acknowledged before William Hopper and N. Wright.

456. 3 December 1748 - 27 September 1750 Richard Bennett from John Coursey - about to depart this Province for England, and for the security of a debt of ₤369.18.6 sterling money of Great Britain; the sum of ₤730.4.2 current money of Maryland and 15,789 pounds of tobacco - and for the maintenance of his family during his absence - conveys to Bennett all real and personal estates. Wit: John Loockerman, Jr. and Thomas Clark. Acknowledged before Richard Tilghman, a Justice

456. of the Provincial Court.

457. 19 September 1750 - 28 September 1750 Mary Coursey, Gentlewoman, to Charles Brown - consideration 5,327 pounds of tobacco - a negro man slave named "James." Wit: Robert Campbell. Acknowledged before Joseph Sudler and Nathan Wright.

458. 26 September 1750 - 8 October 1850 Rachel Duhamel, Spinster, to Richard Hynson, Planter - consideration ₺100 current money - 66 acres, her part of "Wilkinson's Addition" and "Waltham," willed by John Earle Denny to Rachel and Mary Dyre. Acknowledged before William Hopper and Nathan Wright. Alienation fine, one shilling, four pence sterling.

458. 15 September 1750 - 9 October 1750 David Nevil, Planter, to John Allen Wooddell, Planter - consideration ₺112 current money - 150 acres called "Jamaica," lying in Talbot County but now in Queen Anne's, on a branch of Hambleton's Creek in Chester River. Acknowledged to William Hopper and Thomas Hammond. Alienation fine, six shillings sterling, paid to Richard Tilghman.

459. 10 October 1750 - 14 October 1750 James Butler in behalf of Sarah Gutterdge brought a black horse of middle size about twelve years old with a white spot in the middle of his forehead. The owner proving his property and paying the charges may have him. John Downes.

459. 1 May 1750 - 18 October 1750 John Davis, Jr. to Thomas Davis - 68 acres of land called "Addy House," near the Beaverdam Branch of Choptank River - willed by his father Thomas Davis to his nephew Thomas Davis, son of his brother, John Davis, but was made over to me, his son and heir. Acknowledged before William Hopper and Nathan WRight. Alienation fine, two shillings, nine pence sterling.

460. 19 October 1750 Richard Tilghman to Henry Jacobs, Gentleman - in consideration of part of "Sprigley," conveyed by Henry Jacobs to him- gives part of the land whereon Henry Jacobs now dwells (being within a lane of sixty feet wide to be erected by Richard and to be kept up by him, to include a spring opened by Henry Jacobs on Richard's land) - during the natural life of Henry Jacobs. Acknowledged before William Hopper and Nathan Wright.

461. 19 October 1750 Henry Jacobs to Richard Tilghman - in consideration of a sixty-feet lane, conveys "Sprigley" - lying on the river. Acknowledged before William Hopper and Nathan Wright.

461. 10 July 1750 - 24 October 1750 Edward Hall to William Hall - consideration ₺20 - 73¼ acres, part of "Hogg Harbour." Edward and Eleanor his wife (she being first privately examined) acknowledged before N. Wright and John Downes. Alienation fine, two shillings, eleven pence, paid to Richard Tilghman.

462. 15 October 1750 - 25 October 1750 William Hall to John Hall - con-

462. sideration 600 pounds of tobacco - 73¼ acres, part of "Hogg Harbour." William and Luisa his wife (she being first privately examined out of his hearing) acknowledged before N. Wright and John Downes. Alienation fine, two shillings, eleven pence sterling, paid to Richard Tilghman.

463. 17 October 1750 - 25 October 1750 Hynson Wright, Planter, and Sarah his wife, to Richard Costin, Planter - consideration four pistoles, six pieces of eight and ₤21 paper money of Maryland - 100 acres, part of "Tom's Fancy Enlarged" - lying in Tully's Neck, adjoining his Lordship's Manor - east side of Chester Marsh. Hynson and Sarah (she being first privately examined) acknowledged before Nathan Wright and John Downes.

463. 31 August 1750 - 27 October 1750 John Emory, Planter, to Arthur Emory, his brother - a gift of love - 100 acres, part of "Partnership" - adjoining "Emory's Fortune Addition" and a part exchanged with his brother, William Emory - to include the part where Richard Glanding formerly lived. John and Ann his wife (she being first privately examined) acknowledged before James Brown and John Downes.

464. 19 November 1750 - 26 November 1750 Francis Arlett brought a dark iron gray mare about three years old, a star in her forehead - the owner proving his property and paying the charges may have her. John Downes.

464. 4 August 1750 - 26 November 1750 Isaac Ford, Planter, and Mary his wife to Isaiah Wharton of Kent County on Delaware - consideration ₤20 - 100 acres, a parcel of land and marsh in Chester Hundres called "Ford's Chance." Ford gave John Powell and/or John Newnam Power of Attorney to acknowledged his deed in court. Wit: Thomas Jones, James Jones. John Newnam acknowledged before Nathan Wright and N. Wright. Alienation fine, four shillings sterling paid to Richard Tilghman.

465. 24 November 1750 - 27 November 1750 Ernault Hawkins brought a stray mare, chestnut sorrell in colour, a white spot on her forehead, long gray mane, no brand. The owner, proving his property and paying charges, may have her. Thomas Hammond.

465. Brought to be recorded in Queen Anne's County, 27 November 1750. Glamorgan, England - at the April Sessions, 1750 Thomas David Rees was convicted of felony in stealing one white ewe sheep. the property of William Morgan and having received a sentence of death has pleaded for transportation for fourteen years to some of his Majesty's plantations in America - it is so ordered. On the back is written:
Northam, England 8 July 1750 "I, Thomas Benson, Esquire, authorize Mr. Peter Marshall, Master of my Snow "Catherine," to assigne and make over the within convict." Wit: Charles Young.

466. City and County of Bristol, England, 18 June 1750 Philip Davis and

466. Joseph Wells, labourers, convicted of felony, ordered to be transported for fourteen years.
At Gloucester, England, 10 March last, Joseph Dark, Anne Dumm and John Griffiths, convicted of felony, ordered to be transported for seven years - assigned to Benjamin Henning, who assigned to Thomas Benson.
City and County of Bristol, England, 20 November 1749, Elizabeth Falim otherwise Levim, convicted of felony. On 18 December last, Lewis Loddowick, labourer, convicted of felony. On 15 January last, Mary, wife of Griffeth Griffiths, Cordwainer, convicted of felony. On Monday, 22 January, Samuel Tilletts, labourer, convicted of felony; also John Woods, labourer. On 19 March, Arthur Lightfoot and William Borden, labourers, convicted of felony. All ordered to be transported to his Majesty's plantations in America for seven years; assigned to Thomas Benson, who assigned them to Peter Marshall, Master of the Snow "Catherine."

467. City and County of Worcester England, 31 March past, Matthew Rea, convicted of grand larceny, ordered to be transported for seven years. On 15 July last, Abraham Spragg and Richard Wyat, convicted of felony; Abraham Spragg for stealing goods and money in a dwelling house to above the value of fifty shillings; Richard Wyat for sheep stealing - ordered to be transported for fourteen years. Also Jonathon Askew, convicted of felony and being liable to punishment of burning in the hand and Thomas Brittain, convicted of petty larceny and liable to punishment of whipping, have been ordered instead to transportation for seven years. Assigned to Thomas Benson.

468. At Tiverton, County Devon, England, 9 January 1749, Margaret, wife of Peter Crudge, Feltmaker, convicted of felony, ordered to be transported for seven years - assigned to Thomas Benson for passage on the Snow "Catherine," Commander, Peter Marshall.

469. Borough and Parish of Barnstable, County Devon, England, 25 April last, Elizabeth, wife of Richard Moses, Weaver; Mary, wife of William Gould, Weaver; and Mary Jeffery, singlewoman, convicted of felony and ordered to be transported for seven years; assigned to Thomas Benson.

470. Castle of Exon, County Devon, England, 9 January 1749, Joseph Bucknole, Mary Davis, Henry Diment, John Clarke and Catherine Smith, convicted of felony and ordered to be transported for seven years; on 16 April assigned to Thomas Benson.

471. City and County of Gloucester, England, on 5 August past, Ann Ellis, wife of Edward Ellis, convicted of burglary, ordered to be transported for fourteen years; Richard Hobbs, convicted of felony, ordered to be transported for seven years; William Green, convicted of felony, ordered to be transported for fourteen years; John Spencer, convicted of felony, ordered to be transported for seven years. On 10 March last, James Carey, Catherine Lewis, Henry Curks, Kinard Hardar(?), William Davidson, William Oland and Richard Kirby, all

471. convicted of grand larceny, ordered to be transported for seven years, assigned to Benjamin Henning, who assigned them to Thomas Benson of Northam near Biddeford, County Devon, 26 June.

472. At the General Sessions of Gaol Delivery held at Monmouth, County of Monmouth, 3 August past, Rachel Jordan, convicted of felony, ordered to be transported for fourteen years; also on 15 March last, Charles Davis and James Watkins, convicted of felony, ordered to be transported for seven years, were assigned to Benjamin Henning.
At Hereford, County of Hereford, England, 11 March 1748, William Hooper, Thomas Gilbert and Mary Monk, convicted of felony, ordered to be transported for fourteen years.
At Hereford, 29 July last, William Tomkins, convicted of felony, ordered to be transported for seven years; John Parlour, convicted of felony, ordered to be transported for fourteen years. On 17 March last, John Watton, Thomas Watts and Mordecai Ingram, convicted of felony, ordered to be transported for seven years (Thomas Watts since the sentencing is dead). All of the convicts were assigned to Benjamin Henning, who assigned them to Thomas Benson. On 8 July 1750, Benson placed them in the care of Capt. Peter Marshall of the Snow "Catherine."

473. Castle of Taunton, County of Somerset, England, 31 March, Abednego Tackle, John Tackle, William Street, John Toms, Robert Boss, William Watts and John Chilcot, convicted of felony and larceny, ordered to be transported for seven years. Amos Andrews, Thomas Bendall and Jonas Mercer at a former session convicted of felony, ordered to be transported for fourteen years. Robert Butt and Hosea Martin, at Taunton, 31 March, convicted of stealing cloth from the rack, judged to be hanged by the neck until dead, were reprieved and ordered to be transported for seven years.
At the General Quarter Sessions held in the City of Wells, 9 January 1749, in the County of Somerset, Abraham Thatcher, convicted of petty larceny, ordered to be transported for seven years.
At Brewton, County Somerset, 24 April 1750, George Brown convicted of felony, ordered to be transported for seven years. Benjamin Henning contracted with Thomas Benson who assigned them to Peter Marshall for transportation.

475. 5 May 1750 John Meech of Charminster, County Dorset, England, Gent. and Sydenham Williams of Herrington, County Dorset, Esquire, to Thomas Benson of Northam - At a General Gaol Delivery held at Dorchester, County Dorset, 12 March, Richard Forde, Morris Salisbury, William Friford and Elizabeth Hawkins, convicted of felony, were ordered to be transported for seven years; William Noss otherwise Nurse, at a former session convicted of felony, ordered to be transported for fourteen years - all assigned and contracted with Benson for their passage. 8 July 1750 Thomas Benson to Peter Marshall, agreement to transport the felons on board the Snow "Catherine."

All of these Certificates of Gaol Delivery (465-475) were recorded in Queen Anne's County, 27 November 1750.

477. 23 October 1750 - 28 November 1750 Joseph Elliott, Gentleman, to Joseph Pippin - lease of the land called "Newnam's Heritage," 60 acres lying on the east side of Unicorn Branch; for a term of seven years. Pippin to have liberty to cultivate the said lands and make use of timber for necessary repairs. Elliott agrees to repair the dwelling house at his own cost except tendance and accomodation of the workmen. Pippin obliges himself to pay rent of 550 pounds of tobacco and the quitrents per annum and keep all in good repair. Wit: John Seegar, Mary Jackson.

477. 29 November 1750 William Banckes and John Mayne, qualified before Johnathon Nicols to make a just estimate of the annual value of the land belonging to Jacob Boone, orphan of James Boone, deceased - entered upon the land 6 July 1750 and found one dwelling house, 35 by 15 feet, covered with joynted shingles to about 10 feet length and 7 feet deep, with two rooms on a floor - one has a plank floor but is unfinished; an open shed on the east side, 16½ feet long; a kitchen of logg'd saplins, scalpt, 15 feet long, 12 feet wide, covered with clapboards; a logg'd corn house, scalpt saplins, 12 by 8 feet without floor or a door; a logg'd brick shed, scalpt saplins, without a door, 10 feet square; a milk house, framed work, 10 feet square with a plank floor, covered with clapboards; a garden, paled in, 80 feet square; an orchard of 119 apple trees, 77 peach trees and 16 cherry trees; the garden paling and the fences very ordinary. The guardian (NB a woman, not named) allowed to clear certain land so as to square the plantation, cover the tobacco house and kitchen with featheredge shingles or good clapboards and find a pair of hinges for the dwelling house door, also a window shutter for the same; pay quitrents and 400 pounds of tobacco per annum until the orphan shall arrive at an age to possess it.

478. 22 October 1750 - 29 November 1750 Benjamin Hinds and Cornelia his wife, to Gilbert Read - consideration fifteen shillings - conveys one acre of land for the use of a Presbyterian Meeting House and their Society forever, part of "Spread Eagle." Benjamin and Cornelia his wife (she being first privately examined out of his hearing) acknowledged before James Brown and John Seegar. Alienation fine, one-half penny sterling.

479. 21 November 1750 - 29 November 1750 Hamer Ponder, Labourer, to James McCoy, Cordwinder - consideration 4,000 pounds of tobacco - his right to a piece of land known as "Willson's Oldfield," part of "Smith's Delight," containing 100 acres. Acknowledged before James Brown and John Seegar. Alienation fine, four shillings sterling, paid to Richard Tilghman.

480. 17 October 1750 - 30 November 1750 Hynson Wright, Planter, and Sarah his wife, to David Herrington, Planter - consideration ₤25 - 50 acres, called "Beaver Dam," on the east side of the Beaver Dam Branch out of the west side of Great Choptank River. Hynson and Sarah acknowledged before Nathan Wright and John Downes (Sarah being first privately examined). Alienation fine, two shillings sterling.

482. 5 November 1750 - 30 November 1750 John McKonakin and Mary his wife, to Gideon Emory, Planter - consideration ₺150 paper money - 236 acres, part of "McKonakin's Fortune" - beginning at the end of the first line of the "Resurvey of Wood Ridge." John and Mary (she being first privately examined out of hearing of her husband) acknowedged before James Brown and John Seegar, Justices of the Peace. Their signatures - "Meconnikin" appear on the deed. Alienation fine, nine shillings, five pence, half penny sterling, paid to Richard Tilghman.

484. 3 December 1750 ADVERTISEMENT: Now in the possession of the subscriber, a dark bay mare about twelve hands high (gives markings) - whosoever owns her may have, applying as the law directs. Thomas Ringgold.

484. 7 December 1750 ADVERTISEMENT: At the plantation of the subscriber is a middle aged light gray mare about thirteen hands high (gives markings) -the owner desired to come, prove his property and pay the charges and take her away. N. Wright.

484. 2 February 1750 ADVERTISEMENT: John Starkey has taken up as a stray a dark brown mare, full aged, about thirteen hands high - the owner, proving his property and paying the charges may have her again. N. Wright.

484. 21 August 1750 - 31 January 1750 Mary Powel of Kent County (Md.) and Anne Ivye of Kent County, Spinster, great-granddaughter and heir-at-law of Robert Smith, late of Talbot County, to James Tilghman of Talbot County, Attorney at law - consideration ₺40 current money - 400 acres called "Gloster" or "Gloucester," lying at the head of Andover Branch, Chester River. Wit: Richard Tilghman, Samuel Galloway. Acknowledged before Richard Tilghman, Justice of the Provincial Court. Alienation fine, sixteen shillings, sterling.

485. 31 January 1750 Benjamin Kirby to Philemon Emerson of Talbot County - consideration ten shillings current - 42 acres, part of "Stagwell" and 100 acres, "Smeath." Reference made to a Writ of Entry executed at Annapolis the third Tuesday in October last - now released. Acknowledged before Joseph Sudler and John Downes.

486. 15 December 1750 - 7 February 1750 Richard Porter, Jr. Chirurgeon, and Sarah his wife, to William Campbell, Planter - consideration ₺450 current money and 20,000 pounds of tobacco - his dwelling plantation, called "Churnell's Neck," formerly in Talbot County, now in Queen Anne's, in a fork of the eastern branch of Chester River, containing 200 acres - also part of "Annthorpe," originally granted to William Hemsley and sold to Porter by John Hollingsworth, being the residue of the tract sold by John Hollingsworth to William Campbell - also another part of "Annthorpe," 60 acres conveyed to Richard Porter by Nicholas Broadway - lying near Wills Hole, adjoining "Churnell's Neck" on the northeast and adjoining "White Hall" - all of these tracts containing in the whole, 433 acres. Acknowledged before

486. James Brown and Nathan Wright. Alienation fine, eight shillings, three pence sterling, paid to Richard Tilghman.

488. 7 February 1750 William Campbell, Planter, to Thomas Hacket - consideration ₤324 current money - 330 acres called "Providence" - between "Partnership," "Royston" and "Sheppard's Fortune." Acknowledged before William Hopper and Nathan Wright. Alienation fine, thirteen shillings, two pence sterling.

490. 7 February 1750 Peter Maxwell, Joyner, to Thomas Marsh, Gentleman - consideration ₤75 current - a house and lot in Kings Town on Chester River, known as lot Number Three. Peter and Sarah (she being first privately examined) acknowledged before Nathan Wright and John Downes, Jr. Alienation fine, three shillings sterling.

492. 14 February 1750 The ship "Lloyd," Frigate, lying in Shipping Hole, Wye River and having part of her cargo on board, takes in tobacco at ₤7 sterling per tonn freight, consigned to Mr. William Anderson, Merchant, in London. Any gentleman planters or others that are inclined to ship to Anderson, their favours shall be greatfully acknowledged by their humble servant.
NB: As a ship is soon expected from Captain Anderson, if she takes freight under ₤7, I promise to take the same. Samuel Allyne.

492. 28 February 1750 Richard Tilghman, Gentleman, to Nathan Wright, - Jr. - consideration ₤100 current and 5,000 pounds of tobacco - 230 acres called "Content" - lying east of the fresh run that lyes back of the late dwelling house of Thomas Davis, deceased. Acknowledged before Nathan Wright and N. Wright. Alienation fine, nine shillings, two pence, half penny sterling, paid to Richard Tilghman.

493. 16 February 1750 - 7 March 1750 Joseph Slocom (or Slocum), Planter, to Benjamin Roberts - consideration 955 pounds of tobacco and the sum of ₤2.16.0 -two featherbeds and furniture; one large chest; five head of cattle; one mare; a chattel mortgage due on or before 10 November next. Wit: James Brown, Benjamin Blower. Acknowledged before James Brown.

493. 22 February 1750 - 7 March 1750 Thomas Sands and Elizabeth his wife, to Benjamin Roberts - consideration 4,000 pounds of tobacco - 78 acres, part of "Lowe's Desire" - on the north side of Red Lyon Branch - adjoining part sold by George Haddaway to James Roberts. Acknowledged before James Brown and John Seegar. Alienation fine, three shillings, one pence, half penny sterling, paid to Richard Tilghman.

494. 8 March 1750 James Tilghman of Talbot County, Attorney at law, to Matthew Tilghman of Talbot County, Gentleman - consideration five shillings sterling money of Great Britain - 145 acres, part of "Glocester," near Andover Branch - which lies without the lines of an adjacent survey called the "Adventure." Wit: Richard Tilghman, James Earle. James and Anne his wife (she being first privately examined) acknowledged before Richard Tilghman, Justice of Provincial

494. Court. Alienation fine, five shillings, ten pence sterling, paid to Richard Tilghman.

496. 16 February 1750 - 21 March 1750 Henry Lambert and Rachel his wife, William Ford and Elizabeth his wife, Absalom Austin and Jane his wife, to George Powell - Rachel, Elizabeth and Jane being co-heirs of William Teat, deceased - consideration ₤4.7.6 current money of the Province - a tract of land called "Long's Chance," lying on the south side of Hollingsworth's Branch, issuing out of Beaver Dams Branch of Choptank River - containing 50 acres according to a certificate of survey granted to John Long and then sold to William Teat. Acknowledged before James Brown and John Seegar, the said Rachel, Elizabeth and Jane being privately examined out of hearing of their husbands. Alienation fine, two shillings sterling.

497. 10 May 1742 - 30 March 1751 "Received from John Dempster, the sum of ₤120.6.0 current money for the land mortgaged to me by William Shepard, containing 150 acres. Richard Bennett. Test: Robert Lloyd." On 29 March 1751 Robert Lloyd appeared before Jonathon Nicols and made oath that he was at the house of Richard Bennett, Esquire, on 10 May 1742 and saw him sign and deliver to John Dempster the within receipt and at their request he signed his name as a witness to the best of his remembrance. Certified by Jonathon Nicols.

497. 30 March 1751 Phillip Emerson of Talbot County, Gentleman, to John Downes the younger of Talbot County, Gentleman - consideration ₤100 sterling money of Great Britain - 100 acres of land, part of "Smeath," beginning at a bounded red oak mentioned in a release of right of that same part from John King to William Turlo dated 15 March 1697 - also 42 acres, part of "Stagwell," lying on the south side of Price's Cove - bounded on the south side by "Smeath," on the north by the cove, on the west by Wye River. Phillip and Sarah his wife (she being first privately examined) acknowledged before James Brown and William Hopper. Alienation fine, two shillings, eleven pence sterling, paid to Richard Tilghman.

499. 30 March 1751 Evan Lloyd to Richard Tilghman, Gentleman; he becoming special bail for me at suit of Buck's executors - consideration 2,000 pounds of tobacco - four cows and calves; one heifer; two horses; sixteen sheep; my crop of tobacco made last year, save what will pay my rent and all my household goods - a mortgage due on or before 10 September next. Acknowledged before James Brown.

499. 18 November 1750 - 4 April 1751 Jonathon Clarke and Rebecca his wife of Sussex County on Delaware, to Philemon Thomas - consideration 2,666 pounds of tobacco - 66 2/3 acres of land called "Alcock's Pharsalia" - in Tully's Neck, on the main branch of Tuckahoe Creek - adjoining "Hawkins Pharsalia." Wit: John Scott, Stephen Thomas. 17 December 1751 John Scott, Jr. made oath and Stephen Thomas affirmed before N. Wright and John Downes that they saw Jonathon and Rebecca sign a Power of Attorney given to Thomas Lee and John Roe to acknowledge their deed to Philemon Thomas. Alienation fine, two

499. shillings, eight pence sterling, paid to Richard Tilghman. "Rebeckah" Clarke signed the deed thus.

501. 18 November 1750 - 4 April 1751 Jonathon Clarke and Rebecca his wife of Sussex County on Delaware to Stephen Thomas - consideration 1,334 pounds of tobacco - 33 1/3 acres, part of "Alcock's Pharsalia" in Tully's Neck" - adjoining "Hawkins Pharsalia." Wit: John Scott, Stephen Thomas. On the back written: We, Jonathon Clarke and Rebecca Clarke of Sussex County, Province of Pensilvania, have appointed our friends Thomas Lee and John Roe of Queen Anne's County, to acknowledge this deed to Philemon Thomas. 17 December 1750 John Scott, Jr. made oath and Stephen Thomas affirmed, that they saw Jonathon and Rebecca sign the Power of Attorney. John Roe acknowledged before N. Wright and John Downes. Alienation fine, sixteen pence sterling.

503. 5 January 1750 - 30 March 1751 Richard Wells, Jr. of Kent County on Delaware, Practitioner of Physic and Lydia his wife, to William Walls of Kent County, Maryland - consideration £120 lawful money of Maryland - 100 acres, the remaining part of "Bath," being my part purchased of my father, Richard Wells, 27 April 1748 - and the remaining part of "Bath's Addition" adjoining "Bath" - 100 acres purchased of my father - and part of "Bath's Addition," 50 acres bought of my brother Zorababel Wells, 9 June 1748. Richard and Lydia (she being first privately examined) acknowledged before James Brown and John Seegar. Alienation fine, ten shillings sterling.

504. 27 March 1751 - 30 March 1751 Ernault Hawkins, Planter, and Jane his wife, to William Hopper, Gentleman - consideration £115 paper currency of the Province - 256 acres, part of "Conquest," lying in Spaniard's Neck, north side of Corsica Creek - adjoining a part sold to David Register. Ernault and Jane (she being first privately examined) acknowledged before Nathan Wright and N. Wright. Alienation fine, ten shillings, three pence sterling, paid to Richard Tilghman.

507. FOR LONDON - the Brigantine "Princess," Thomas Jones, Commander, now lying at Chester Town, Chester River, takes on freight at £7 sterling per tonn with liberty of consignment to any merchant in London for freight or passage; agree with Mr. Daniel Surrell or the said Commander at Chester Town. She hath good accomodations for passengers. NB: She will sail by the middle of May having the best part of her cargo engaged. Thomas Jones.

507. 30 March 1751 ADVERTISEMENT: This day Samuel Massey brought before me a full aged roan horse, fourteen hands high (gives other markings) the owner is ordered to come and take him. N. Wright.

507. 27 March 1751 - 30 March 1751 William Hopper to Ernault Hawkins and Jane his wife, Planters - lease of part of "Conquest" (being old field), lying between Peter Falcom's house and the tract "Bramton." (no acreage given). From this date during their natural lives, paying yearly one good chicken pye on Lady Day on demand. Acknowledged

507. before N. Wright, Solomon Wright.

508. 23 March 1750 - 30 March 1750 John Roe and Samuel Roe, qualified by N. Wright to make just estimate of the annual value of the lands of Benjamin Chaires, a minor under the care of Rebecca Chaires, Widow and guardian - on 20 December last, entered unto the land and found on the plantation in occupation of Samuel French (part of "Warplesdon Addition" and part of his Lordship's Mannor), one logg house, 20 by 16 feet; one other logg house, 12 by 12 feet; one small corn house, not worth repairing; two tobacco houses 30 by 20 feet in midling good repair; a young orchard and other scattering fruit trees; the fencing in good repair. The guardian not to clear or cut timber except for necessary repairs; the value estimated at 550 pounds of tobacco per annum exclusive of quitrents and necessary repairs.

508. 23 March 1750 - 30 March 1750 John Roe and Samuel Roe, qualified by N. Wright to make just estimate of the annual value of the lands of Joseph Chaires, a minor under the care of Rebecca Chaires, Widow and guardian - on 20 December last, entered and found on the plantation occupied by Mary Kemp (part of "Lently") one small logg house, not worth repairing; some old scattered fruit trees; the fencing about all rotten; the guardian not to clear or cut timber except for necessary repairs; the value estimate at 350 pounds of tobacco per annum exclusive of quitrents and necessary repairs.

509. 18 October 1850 - 30 March 1751 Jacob Bromwell of Talbot County, Innholder, to Nathan Samuel Turbutt Wright, Gentleman - release of a Writ of Entry obtained at a Provincial Court held 16 May 1749, Bromwell versus Nathan Samuel Turbutt Wright on the land "Warplesdon," formerly in Talbot now in Queen Annes County in a fork of Elliott's Branch, 300 acres, and "Solomon's Friendship," 100 acres in Elliott's Branch adjoining his Lordship's Mannor and the lands of Solomon Wright. Nathan Samuel Turbutt Wright did warranty unto Richard Goldsmith of Ann Arundel County who warranted unto Jacob Bromwell and after made default and recovery was made. Wit: Nicholas Glen, Solomon Coursey Wright.
TALBOT COUNTY - Jacob Bromwell acknowledged before Thomas Bozman and James Edge - certified by John Leeds, Clerk of Talbot County.

510. 13 March 1750 - 30 March 1751 Joshua Jacobs to Dr. Sluyter Bouchell of Cecil County - consideration ₤26.18.6 current money of Maryland - one bay horse, eight years old; four cows; two heifers; one bull yearling; four ewes; ten hoggs; nine piggs - a mortgage due on or before 1 September next. Acknowledged before John Seegar.

511. 26 January 1750 - 4 April 1751 Thomas Richardson Roe and Margaret his wife, to George Baynard - consideration 10,030 pounds of tobacco and ₤12 current money - 147 acres of land, part of "Roe's Chance," lying in Tully's Neck. Acknowledged before Nathan Wright and N. Wright. Alienation fine, five shillings, ten pence, half penny sterling paid to Richard Tilghman.

512. 20 March 1750 - 4 April 1751 William Scott, Planter, and Lucrecie his wife, to Joseph Elliott, Planter - consideration 5,000 pounds of tobacco - 60 acres of land, part of "Sayer's Range," on the south side of Red Lyon Branch. Acknowledged by William and Lucrecie (she being first privately examined) before Joseph Sudler and John Seegar.

514. 26 October 1750 - 4 April 1751 Jonathon Nicols and Mary his wife, to Charles Nicols - a tract of land called "Jones'es Forrest," on the east side of Tuckahoe Creek, containing 500 acres; in exchange for part of "Partnership," now possessed by Charles Nicols, on the west side of Tuckahoe Creek - between the part belonging to Jeremiah Nicols of Talbot County and part belonging to Jonathon Nicols. Acknowledged before N. Wright and John Downes. Alienation fine, twenty four shillings, three pence sterling.

516. 1 April 1751 - 4 April 1751 Richard Hynson, Planter, to Rachel Duhamel - consideration ₤100 current money - 199 acres, part of "Hynson's Lott" - at the mouth of Horsepen Branch. Richard and Ann his wife (she being first privately examined out of his hearing) acknowledged before Nathan Wright and N. Wright.

517. 19 March 1750 - 4 April 1751 Anne Ivey of Kent County (Md.), singlewoman, to John Wallace of Chester Town, Merchant - consideration ₤32.5.0 current money - 300 acres of land called "Triangle Addition," lying on the north side of Corsica Creek, heretofore in Talbot but now in Queen Annes County, originally laid out for Robert Smith - bounded by "Triangle;" Peterson's land; land now or lately in the possession of John Hart; the land of Richard Jones, Jr., formerly laid out for "Jones's Farm;" the land of Robert Norris, formerly laid out for Jonathon Sybrey and the land of George Pascall. Wit: Charles Scott, W. Hynson. Anne Ivey acknowledged before Charles Scott, a Justice of the Peace for Kent County, certified by James Smith, Clerk of Kent County. Alienation fine, twelve shillings sterling paid to Richard Tilghman.

519. 4 April 1751 - 11 April 1751 John Toomy, Carpenter, to William Elbert - consideration ₤20 current money - one sorrell mare called "Fly;" one bay mare, two years old; one cow and yearling; two cows; two pewter dishes; nine plates; one featherbed, two blankets and a rugg, with a bedsted; one smaller featherbed with two blankets and bedsted; one small iron pott - a mortgage due on or before 10 October next. Wit: Thomas Hammond, Macklin Elbert. Acknowledged before Thomas Hammond.

520. 14 January 1750 - 18 April 1751 John Cole of Talbot County, Wheelwright and Anna his wife, to James Toalson - consideration ₤15 current - their part of 359 acres called "Oak Ridge" and 150 acres called "Hiccory Ridge." Acknowledged before Jonathon Nicols and John Downes. Alienation fine, five shillings sterling paid to Richard Tilghman.

521. 3 April 1751 - 18 April 1751 This day Jeremiah Grasingham brought a dark roan mare about five hands high - the owner proving his property and paying the costs can have her. John Downes.

521. 20 April 1751 - 24 April 1751 Thomas Stevens brought before me a small sorrell horse, a stray. The owner, proving his property and paying costs can have her. Thomas Hammond.

521. 24 January 1750 - 25 April 1751 Edward Brown and Ann his wife, to John Nabb - consideration ₤53 - 150 acres, part of "Tom's Fancy Enlarged," adjoining the lands of Charles Lizenbe, John Lloyd, Hynson Wright and Nathaniel Read. Acknowledged before Nathan Wright and John Downes. Alienation fine, six shillings sterling paid to Richard Tilghman.

523. 13 March 1750 - 2 May 1751 Thomas Butler, Planter, to Charles Browne, Merchant - consideration 2,000 pounds of tobacco - 50 acres of land called "Butler's Owne" - on the Long Marsh. Thomas and Sarah his wife (she being first privately examined) acknowledged before William Hopper and Nathan Wright. Alienation fine, two shillings sterling.

524. 7 May 1751 John Ally, Planter, to Richard Tilghman - consideration 8,000 pounds of tobacco - five cows and calves; three 2-year old heifers; one 4-year old steer; one 2-year old steer; one cow and yearling; fifteen ewes; fourteen lambs; one ram; two weathers; one white plow horse; one bay mare and sorrel yearling colt; one blaze mare and blaze mare colt; one young sorrel horse; two featherbeds and furniture; one desk, and all of my household furniture; the crop of tobacco made last year - a mortgage due on or before the last day of July next. Acknowledged before William Hopper.

525. 30 April 1751 - 7 May 1751 James Cox, Clerk(?), to John Jackson, Physician - consideration five shillings sterling - 27 acres of land a part of "Adventure," lying north of the main road that leads from Chester Church to Queens Town - beginning at a post by the Church, the beginning also of Dodd's land. Acknowledged before William Hopper and Nathan Wright. Alienation fine, thirteen pence sterling.

526. 13 May 1751 - 14 May 1751 John Sartain and Mabel his wife, to Francis Rochester - consideration ₤130 paper currency - 175 acres, all of "Collins' Gift," a part formerly called "Smith's Range Addition," lying on the south side of the Southeast Branch of Chester River - adjoining "Ripley," formerly laid out for Stephen Tully. Acknowledged before James Brown and John Seegar. Alienation fine, seven shillings sterling.

528. 17 April 1751 - 15 May 1751 James Hutchins to Thomas Elliott Hutchins - consideration the yearly rents - a parcel of land on Red Lyon Branch called "Condon," for a term of ten years - the yearly rent one ear of Indian corn and the quitrents. Wit: John Brice, N. Wright. Acknowledged before John Brice.

529. 20 March 1750 - 23 May 1751 William Scott, Planter, and Lucrecie his wife, to Benajmin Roberts, Planter - consideration ₺100 current - 100 acres of land, part of "Sawyer's Range" - lying on the south side of Red Lyon Branch. Acknowledged by William and Lucrecie (she being first privately examined out of hearing of her husband) before Joseph Sudler and John Seegar. Alienation fine, four shillings sterling, paid to Richard Tilghman.

531. 1 June 1751 - 3 June 1751 John Offley Collins, Planter, to John Smyth of Kent Island, Chirurgion - consideration ₺150 current money and 16,000 pounds of tobacco - 200 acres of land, part of "Spread Eagle" - near the head of the Southeast Branch, Chester River, and on the south side of Collins' Millpond and Collins' Mill Branch - also the mill, millhouse, mill damm, pond and mill lands on the head of the Southeast Branch of Chester River, commonly called Collins' Mill - and five acres adjoining, excepted out of a parcel sold by John Collins, father of John Offley Collins, to Rachel Meloyd. John Offley Collins and Sarah his wife (she being first privately examined) acknowledged before James Brown and Nathan Wright. Alienation fine, eight shillings, two pence sterling.

532. 6 June 1751 John Clayland, Sr., Gentleman, to his sons, John and James Clayland - consideration of his love and affection - 300 acres, his part of "Trustram" on Wye River. Wit: Richard Tilghman, James Emory. Acknowledged before Richard Tilghman, Justice of the Provincial Court. Alienation fine, six shillings sterling.

534. 27 March 1751 - 20 June 1751 John Allin Wooddell and Mary his wife, to Robert Walters - consideration ₺100 current money - 200 acres, all of "Jamaica" and part of "Mt. Hope" - on the branches of Hambleton's Creek. Acknowledged before Joseph Sudler and John Downes, Jr. Alienation fine, eight shillings sterling.

535. 3 May 1751 - 20 June 1751 James Ponder of Newcastle County (Dela), Farmer, to James Ware - consideration ₺80 current money - 112½ acres, part of "Clouds' Adventure" - lying on the south side of Hambleton's Branch. James and Mary his wife (she being first privately examined) acknowledged before James Brown and William Hopper. Alienation fine, four shillings, six pence sterling.

Here ends Volume R. T. C 1743 - 1751

SOME QUEEN ANNE COUNTY PATENTS

TOWTONFIELDS ADDITION - 140 acres, surveyed 21 July 1732 for William Hemsley - beginning at a bounded stooping chestnut tree on the south side of the Horsehead Branch and in the south line of Towtonfields. (Patents, Vol. A.M. #1 f.14)

CHESTNUT RIDGE - 200 acres, surveyed 5 August 1732 for Burton Francis Falconer and John Falconer - lying on the drains of the French Woman's Branch - on the west side of the road that leads from Tully's Neck to Tuckahoe Bridge. (Patents, Vol. A.M. #1 f.16)

MEREDITH'S ADVENTURE CORRECTED - 71 acres, surveyed 7 October 1758 for Richard Harrison. A resurvey of Meredith's Adventure, granted 26 May 1723 to John Meredith - with vacant land added. (Patents, Vol. BC & GS #11 f.269)

ADVENTURE - 50 acres on Kent Island granted to William Legg, 5 May 1680. Surveyed and laid out 10 August 1684 and assigned to Lewis Meredith. (Patents, Vol. 22 f.14)

NOBLE'S RANGE - 200 acres, surveyed 1 July 1679 for Robert Noble, in a fork of Williams' Branch. 33 acres, possessed by Henry Costin; 167 acres by John Brown. (Rent Rolls #12 f. 339)

ST. MARTIN'S - 100 acres, on Tuckahoe Creek, surveyed __ July 1666, for Thomas Goddard. (Patents, Vol. #9 f.125)

MANGY POCKEY - 100 acres, surveyed 20 May 1705 for Nathaniel Cleave of Kent County (Md.) - in the woods near the Long Marsh. (Patents, Vol. D.D. #5 f.568)

HIGHGATE - 50 acres, on the west side of Island Creek - assigned to Michael Hackett out of a warrant for 300 acres granted to Henry Parker, 13 February 1679 - surveyed 4 March 1679. (Patents, Vol. 21 f.229)

HACKETT'S DELIGHT - 150 acres, surveyed for Michael Hackett - on the west side of the Delaware Road. 4 March 1679 (Patents, Vol. 21 f.229)

TRUSTRAM - 1300 acres, comprised of "Trustram" and "Trustram's Addition," originally resurveyed for Trustram Thomas, with added vacancy. Thomas devised the 1300 acres to his several sons, i.e. 300 acres each to his sons Thomas and Christopher; 233 acres each to his sons William, Stephen and Trustram Thomas. (Patents, BY & GS #1 f.347 29 Sept. 1748)

DUNGARNON - 300 acres, surveyed 12 August 1687 for Flowrence Sullivane - on the Red Lyon Branch in Chester River. (Rent Rolls #12 f. 402)

BRADFORD - 100 acres, patented 28 July 1678 for John Broadribb of Talbot County. On the south side of Chester River, northeast side of John Elliott's Branch. (Patents #21 f. 118)

QUEEN ANNE COUNTY LAND RECORDS - R. T. D 1751 - 1755

Page

001. 24 June 1751 Thomas Hammond to Richard Tilghman - consideration ₤51.6.0 - his reversionary interest in "Cheshire" and "The Plains." Acknowledged before William Hopper and Nathan Wright.

001. 24 June 1751 Thomas Hammond to Richard Tilghman - consideration ₤40 sterling - 75 acres of land, part of "Gray's Inn," bought of Richard and Rachel Jones. Thomas and Elizabeth his wife (she being first privately examined out of hearing of her husband) acknowledged before William Hopper and Nathan Wright.

003. 24 June 1751 Joseph Sudler, Esquire, Chief Justice of Queen Anne County Court, to Henry Jacobs - reference made to an Act of Assembly empowering Justices to sell the materials of the old prison of that county - in consideration of the sum of ₤55 current money - the old prison standing in Queens Town and one-fourth part of an acre of land where it standeth - near the easternmost corner of the old prison on Courthouse Street. Acknowledged before Richard Tilghman.

004. 30 May 1751 - 24 June 1751 John Woodall and Elizabeth his wife of Kent County (Md.) to Henry Callister - consideration ₤65 current money - part of "Sandy Husk" - lying between the mouth of Red Lyon Branch and the mouth of Pearle's Creek. Acknowledged by John and Elizabeth (she being first privately examined) before James Brown and John Seegar. Alienation fine, ten shillings sterling, paid to Richard Tilghman.

005. 30 May 1741 - 24 June 1751 John Woodall and Elizabeth his wife of Kent County (Md.) to Henry Callister - consideration ₤100 current money - 200 acres of land called "Grompton" - on Red Lyon Branch. John and Elizabeth (she being first privately examined) acknowledged before James Brown and John Seegar. Alienation fine, eight shillings sterling.

006. 24 June 1751 - 25 June 1751 Jacob Alquire, Planter, to Henry Lizenberry, Planter - consideration ₤75 current money - 115 acres of land, part of "Parson's Chance" - adjoining "Tilghman's Discovery" and on Beckles' Creek. Acknowledged before James Brown and John Seegar. Alienation fine, four shillings, seven pence sterling.

007. 25 March 1751 - 11 July 1751 John Tharp and Elizabeth his wife, of Kent County on Dillawar, Planter, to Daniel Cox of Dorchester County, Carpenter - consideration ₤22 - 25 acres of land, part of "Cole Rain" - lying on the west side of Tuckahoe Creek, on the sorth side of Kittemore's Branch. John and Elizabeth acknowledged before N. Wright and John Downes (Elizabeth being first privately examined). Alienation fine, one shilling sterling.

008. 9 May 1751 - 23 July 1751 William Coursey, Gentleman, of the first part; John Cole, Wheelwright, and Anna his wife, of the second part

008. and Richard Small, Planter - in consideration of the sum of ₤140 current money - 150 acres of land called "Cole's Endeavour" - patented to William Cole, 23 May 1729 - William Coursey to have a recovery in the land. Acknowledged before John Downes and John Downes, Jr. (Anna, wife of John Cole being first privately examined).

010. 1 June 1751 - 23 July 1751 Robert Gwinn, Planter, to John Seegar, Planter - consideration 5,000 pounds of tobacco - 100 acres called "Gwin's Hazard" - lying on the east side of Unicorne Branch - adjoining "Woodhouse Addition." Robert and Mary his wife (she being first privately examined out of his hearing) acknowledged before James Brown and Nathan Wright. Alienation fine, four shillings sterling paid to Richard Tilghman.

011. 22 July 1751 - 23 July 1751 Stephen Wickes, Planter, to Henry Lizenby, Planter - consideration 8,000 pounds of tobacco - 84 acres of land, sold by James Earle and William Turbutt towards the payment of the debts of Robert Smith, to John Wickes, father of Stephen - part of two tracts lying on the east side of Double Creek - one, "Mt. Pleasure" alias "Mt. Pleasant;" the other, "Enjoyment" alias "Lillingston's Enjoyment." Stephen and Ann his wife (she being first privately examined) acknowledged before James Brown and John Seegar. Alienation fine, three shillings, four pence, half penny sterling.

013. 11 July 1741 - 24 July 1751 Benjamin Hinds, Planter, to Andrew Hall - consideration ₤15 current money - 149 acres, part of "Spread Eagle," lying on the Southeast Branch of Chester River. Benjamin and Cornelia his wife (she being first privately examined out of his hearing) acknowledged before James Brown and John Seegar. Alienation fine, six shillings sterling.

015. 15 July 1751 - 24 July 1751 Bartholomew Jadwin, Planter, to Charles Brown, Merchant - consideration 1,500 pounds of tobacco - 50 acres of land called "Piney Swamp" - on the west side of the northernmost branch of Choptank River - near the head of Bee Tree Swamp. Acknowledged before Richard Tilghman, Justice of the Provincial Court. Alienation fine, two shillings sterling.

016. 22 July 1751 - 24 July 1751 Thomas Bostick and Samuel Bostick, Planters, to Gideon Swift, Planter - consideration 3,150 pounds of tobacco - 100 acres, all of "Northumberland" - lying between the Red Lyon and the Unicorne Branches. Acknowledged before James Brown and John Seegar. Alienation fine, four shillings sterling.

017. 20 July 1751 - 25 July 1751 Edward Couzens of Kent County (Md.), Planter, and Elizabeth his wife; Abraham Ambrose, Planter, and Robena his wife (daughter of Robert Green of Kent County, deceased), to Francis Rochester, Planter - consideration ₤27.10.0 current - 200 acres, part of "Outrange," formerly in Talbot, now in Queen Anne County, near the head of a small branch of Hamilton's Creek, Chester River. Acknowledged before Bedingfield Hands and Charles Scott, Justices of the Peace for Kent County (Elizabeth and Robena private-

017. ly examined). Alienation fine, three shillings, two pence, half-penny sterling, paid to Richard Tilghman.

018. 3 May 1751 - 25 July 1751 James Earle of Kent County, Delaware, Planter, to Matthew Tilghman of Talbot County (Md.), Gentleman - consideration ₺390 current money - the "Ovall," lying in the fork of Tuckahoe, taken up in the name of Thomas Thomas, deceased, for 355 acres of land, but since surveyed by James Earle with added vacancy for 420 acres. Also part of "Tom's Fancy Enlarged," 162 acres, bought by James Earle of Thomas Hynson Wright, deceased - adjoining John Atkinson's part of the said land. James and Anne his wife (she being first privately examined) acknowledged before Jonathon Nicols and N. Wright. Alienation fine, ₺1.3.3½ sterling.

020. 10 July 1751 - 25 July 1751 Charles Stant, Planter, to Daniel Baker, Planter - consideration ₺8.4.0 paper currency - one gray mare, 3 years old; two iron potts; one set shoemaker's tools; one English Bible - a mortgage - Charles Stant to pay Robert Lloyd ₺8.4.0 in paper currency for which Daniel Baker has been bound, on or before 1 March 1751. Wit: Nathan Baker, John Falkner, Jonathon Nicols.

021. 26 July 1751 George Smith and N. Wright, Jr., qualified by N. Wright to make estimate of the value of "Upper Deale," the right of Mary and Elizabeth Evans and Anne Price, minors and co-heiresses, under the care of Benjamin Kirby, their guardian - on 27 April last, entered upon the land and found one plantation, occupied by Alice Wright, with one clapboard dwelling house, 20 by 15 feet wanting repairing; one tobacco house, rough work, 40 by 20 feet, wanting repairing; one small orchard; the fencing about the plantation in good repair; the guardian to clear fifteen acres of woodland. On the plantation occupied by Walter Edwards, one old dwelling house, 25 by 22 feet; one other dwelling house, 16 by 12 feet; one tobacco house, 40 by 20 feet; one corn house; all wanting repair; the fencing in poor repair. The guardian permitted to clear 10 acres of woodland, with liberty to cut timber for necessary repairs; the annual value, 1,300 pounds of tobacco clear of quitrents and necessary repairs.

021. 11 July 1751 - 26 July 1751 Peter Johnson, Planter, to Richard Warner, Planter - consideration ₺100 current money - part of "Sawyer's Addition," 66 acres on Little Red Lyon Branch; part of "Albert's Desire," 40 acres adjoining "Sawyer's Addition." Peter and Mary his wife (she being first privately examined) acknowledged before James Brown and John Seegar. Alienation fine, four shillings, three pence sterling, paid to Richard Tilghman.

023. 8 July 1751 - 26 July 1751 Edward Cahill, Planter, to William Anderson, Jonathon Nicols & Company - consideration ₺10 current money - one gray gelding named "Buttock," about seven years old; one black mare named "Pleasure," about seven years old; three cows and one yearling bull. Wit: William Bowness, John Fownes. Acknowledged before John Downes.

024. 17 May 1751 - 27 July 1751 John Allen Woodall, Planter, to Charles Browne, Merchant - consideration ₤44.3.1 paper currency - 312 acres of land lying in Hamilton's Branch of Chester River, called "Hope." A mortgage due on or before 16 May 1752. Wit: Jo. Smith, Robert Campbell. Acknowledged before Richard Tilghman, Justice of the Provincial Court. Alienation fine, twelve shillings, six pence sterling paid to Richard Tilghman.

025. 24 July 1751 - 27 July 1751 John Seegar, Gentleman, to Alexander Toulson, Planter - a division of 424½ acres of land called "Partnership," owned jointly - Tolson to Seegar, 150¼ acres; Seegar to Toulson, 139½ acres. Acknowledged before John Downes and Thomas Hammond.

026. 27 July 1751 Alexander Toulson to John Seegar - a divison of their land called "Partnership" - lying in the fresh runns of Island Creek - conveyed to Seegar, 150¼ acres. Acknowledged before John Downes and Thomas Hammond.

028. 26 July 1751 Henry Feddeman and Hawkins Downes, qualified by Jonathon Nicols to view and value the estate of Henry Sharp, orphan of William Sharp - on 13 April 1751 entered upon the land and found two dwelling houses of saplin round loggs, covered with clapboards in good repair; one tobacco house, 30 feet long, framed work, covered with clapbords in good repair; one apple orchard of forty small trees. All fences in good repair. The guardian to clear fifty acres and keep the orchard inclosed in a good fence; build a dwelling house, 24 by 16 feet, well covered with good featheredged shingles and framed work; pay the quitrents and pay the orphan at age twenty-one 500 pounds of tobacco for each year.

028. 27 July 1751 Marmaduke Goodhand and John Smith, qualified by John Downes to view and value a tract of land on Kent Island, known as "Broad Creek," the right of Ann Wells, a minor, her guardian Captain Joseph Sudler - on 5 April 1751 entered upon the land and found one large brick dwelling house, two rooms on a floor, above and below, plaistered, the partitions and mantil pieces of wainscott; a cellar the whole length of the house, it being forty feet in length, out of repair; one old 40 by 20 feet tobacco house; another tobacco house 25 by 20 feet, neither worth repairing; one 15 feet logg house; another, 20 by 16 feet; one logg corn house, one kitchin 26 by 16 feet, brick gable end and chimley(sic!), very much out of repair; one milk house, 8 feet square. There is on the plantation 1,725 pannells of fence; 100 old apple trees - the annual value ₤15 paper currency - the guardian to get timber for repairs and build such new houses as are wanting and new fences. He is permitted to clear in the Church Old Field and clear all woods within the fence; also the woods from the head of Gravelly Run to the main road that goes to Love Point, with the said road to the corner of the Church Old Field and from the corner to a small hill where formerly a tenement was intended, and with a straight line from the hill to the Church. Joseph Sudler, Guardian.

029. 15 August 1751 - 27 August 1751 Nathan Wright, Jr., son and heir of Edward Wright, deceased, to Charles Browne, Merchant - consideration 3,140 pounds of tobacco - 50 acres of land called "Canaan," lying between the branches of Choptank River and Tuckahoe - on the road which formerly led from the head of Choptank to Chester. Nathan, Jr. and Mary his wife (she being first privately examined out of his hearing) acknowledged before William Hopper and Nathan Wright. Alienation fine two shillings sterling paid to Richard Tilghman.

030. 4 May 1751 - 31 August 1751 Samuel Austin and John Watson to each other - an agreement - John Watson from Samuel Austin, 100 acres of land, part of two tracts, (1) "Bishop's Addition" and (2) "Bishop's Outlet," given by Mrs. Alice Collier to Margaret Carter - Watson agrees that Samuel Austin is to have the reaminder of the two tracts. Wit: Thomas Wilkinson, Mary Wilkinson.

031. 31 August 1751 Edward Brown, Jr. and Charles Connor, qualified and sworn before Joseph Sudler, Esquire, to view and value the land called "Sillin" on Kent Island, belonging to Mary Evans and Elizabeth Evans and Anne Price, minors, their guardian, Benjamin Kirby - on 13 April 1751 entered upon the land and found one dwelling house, 24 by 16 feet, brick chimney and shed adjoining, 24 by 12 feet, brick chimney, out of repair; one tobacco house, 40 by 20 feet, indifferent good; one kitchen, 16 by 12 feet, good; one logg corn house, not worth repairing; one lower frame of a tobacco house, worth repairing; one 16-feet house, wants covering; one tobacco house, 30 by 22 feet; one old logg corn house not worth repairing; one old gum logg house on the said plantation; 1,386 pannells of fencing; 46 sorry apple trees - the annual value 1,500 pounds of tobacco. The guardian to get timber for repairs and building new tobacco houses and fences; and to clear all the ground within the fences as it now stands.

031. 28 August 1751 - 31 August 1751 Thomas Baley, Planter, to John Watson and Esther his wife - consideration ₤30 current money and 500 pounds of tobacco - 100 acres of land, all of my part of "Baley's Delight," whereon I now live. Thomas and Esther his wife (she being first privately examined) acknowledged before N. Wright and John Seegar. Alienation fine, four shillings sterling, paid to Richard Tilghman.

032. 30 August 1751 - 31 August 1751 Samuel Austin to James Ringgold of Eastern Neck in Kent County (Md.), Gentleman - consideration ₤60 - 78 acres called "Coursey's Point" alias "Smith's Mistake," on the north side of Corsica Creek, that William Bishop and his wife sold to John Austin, father of said Samuel Austin. Samuel and Mary his wife (she being first privately examined) acknowledged before John Downes, Jr. and N. Wright. Alienation fine, three shillings, one pence, half penny sterling.

034. 30 August 1751 - 31 August 1751 Jacob Bayley, Planter, to James Ringgold of Eastern Neck, Kent County (Md.) - consideration 4,500 pounds

034. of tobacco and ₺5 current money - 200 acres on the north side of Coursica Creek called "Bishop's Outlett" - sold by William Bishop to Jacob Bayley, father of the grantor - also 50 acres adjoining a part of the said land bought by James Ringgold of Nathan and Thomas Wright. Acknowledged before John Downes, Jr. and John Seegar. Alienation fine, two shillings sterling, paid to Richard Tilghman.

035. 28 August 1751 - 31 August 1751 John Watson, Planter, to James Ringgold of Eastern Neck in Kent County (Md.) - consideration ₺36 current money and 1,000 pounds of tobacco - 100 acres of land, part of "Bishop's Outlett" and part of "Bishop's Addition" - adjoining "Coursey's Point." John and Esther his wife (she being first privately examined out of his hearing) acknowledged before Jonathon Nicols and John Seegar. Alienation fine, four shillings sterling.

037. 5 September 1751 Nathan Samuel Turbutt Wright to Sarah Reed, wife of Nathaniel Reed - consideration 5,000 pounds of tobacco paid by Nathaniel Reed to Thomas Hynson Wright in his lifetime - 100 acres, part of "Wright's Square" - adjoining Nathaniel Reed's part of "Tom's Fancy Enlarged." Wit: Thomas Wright, Francis Barnes. Acknowledged before Richard Tilghman, Justice of the Provincial Court.

038. 7 September 1751 Richard Kieran brought an iron gray mair (sic!) about three years old, no brand, a switch tail - the owner may apply to Richard Kieran, living in Bee Tree Neck, and proving property and paying costs can have her. John Seegar.

038. 10 September 1751 - 11 September 1751 William Greenwood to William Coursey and John Tillotson - consideration ₺1,000 current money - fifteen negroes, vizt: "Jack Towerhill," "Benny," "Pompey," "Young Jack," "George," "Jacob," "Nann," "Priss," "Sarah," "Rachel," "Cate," "Jenny," "Bess," and "Phillis;" all my horses, mares and colts; sixty head of cattle; sixty head of sheep; 100 head of hoggs and all my household goods and furniture. Acknowledged before William Hopper and John Downes, Jr.

039. 5 September 1751 - 12 September 1751 John Baily and Mary Smith Baily, his wife, late of Queen Anne County but now of Newcastle County in Pensilvania, to Ernault Hawkins - consideration ₺10 current money - one negro boy named "Polydore" - given by Ernault Hawkins to Mary Andrew, now wife of John Baily. Wit: Thomas Hammond, Mary Stinson. Acknowledged before Thomas Hammond.

039. 10 September 1751 - 12 September 1751 William Greenwood to Jane Lock, his housekeeper, for sundry services performed - one negro girl named "Doll," which now lives with Jane's sister in Chester Town in Kent County, named Eleanor Hollyday. Wit: John Tillotson, Thomas Wilkinson. Acknowledged before John Downes, Jr.

040. 2 September 1751 - 14 September 1751 William Elbert and William Kent, qualified before Thomas Hammond to estimate and value the land of John Brown, an orphan, entered upon the land and found one hundred acres, about fifty or sixty cleared, the most part under reasonably good fencing; one old dwelling house, 38 feet long, 16 feet wide, with brick gable ends and chimneys, plank floor and a small shed on the back side about 15 feet long; one large kitchen, 28 feet long, 15 feet wide with a stack of chimneys in the middle, no loft, with a single cover of boards and old; one meat house, 12 feet long, 10 feet wide, covered with boards, in good order; one hewed logg corn house, 12 feet long, 8 feet wide, covered with shingles and in good order; one barn, 33 feet long, 20 feet wide, whole fraimd, about 12 feet pitch, shingled and in good order except the doors; an old brick oven; an orchard of apple trees, thirteen in length and eleven in width, a few missing, ordered; seven large cherry trees; nine pare (sic!) trees; six young English Walnut trees; a small peach orchard and but a few now alive; about fifty small apple trees in a nursery; no more than two acres to be cleared yearly of the woodlin (sic!) land; the yearly rent, 500 pounds of tobacco.

040. 22 September 1751 On 20 September John Seney brought before me a middle sized white horse, taken as a stray; seems to be old. Thomas Hammond.

040. 8 April 1751 - 26 September 1751 John Ruth, Planter, to Samuel McCosh, Weaver - consideration 16,000 pounds of tobacco and ₤55 current money - 50 acres, part of "Heath's Forrest," lying on the west side of the Southwest Branch of Island Creek - given in 1702 by James Heath to Thomas Ruth, father of the said John, in exchange of a parcel of land called "Crump's Forrest" - 53 acres, all of "Heath's Gift," adjoining "Larrington," "Plaindealing" and "Bishop's Outlet." Also part of "Larrington als Lavington" - lying on the west side of the Southwest Branch of Island Creek, containing 118 acres. Acknowledged before James Brown and Nathan Wright. Alienation fine, eight shillings, nine pence sterling, paid to Richard Tilghman.

042. 7 October 1751 ADVERTISEMENT: The Snow, "Nancy," lying in Wye River and shortly bound to Chester and from thence to London, will take tobacco on board at the rate of ₤7 per tonn, consigned to William Anderson, Merchant. James Henderson.

042. 22 May 1751 - 7 October 1751 Reuben Taylor of Kent County on Delaware in Little Creek Hundred, to Nathan Samuel Turbutt Wright and Thomas Wright, Gentlemen - consideration ₤30 current money - 76 acres, part of "Lowe's Arcadia" - adjoining Robert Certain's part; Samuel Taylor's part, lately conveyed to Thomas Hynson Wright; a part lately in possession of John Pickerine(?) and a part now or lately possessed by Thomas Shoebrook and David Phillips. Wit: John Atkinson, John Wright. Acknowledged before William Hopper and Nathan Wright. Alienation fine, three shillings, nine pence sterling.

044. 10 August 1751 - 7 October 1751 Thomas Wright, Gentleman, to Nathan Samuel Turbutt Wright - consideration ₤50 current money - 240 acres, part of "Larrington," "Kendall" and "Wright's Square." Acknowledged before William Hopper and Nathan Wright. Alienation fine, nine shillings, seven pence, half penny sterling, paid to Richard Tilghman.

045. 10 August 1751 - 7 October 1751 Nathan Samuel Turbutt Wright to Thomas Wright - consideration ₤250 current - 907 acres, part of "Soloman's Friendship," "Warplesdon," "Warplesdon Addition" and "Lowe's Arcadia." Acknowledged before William Hopper and Nathan Wright. Alienation fine, ₤1.16.3.½ sterling.

047. 11 October 1751 - 17 October 1751 Thomas Hammond, Planter, to Charles Browne, Merchant - consideration 9,000 pounds of tobacco and ₤1.10.0 current money - all of the tobacco I have on my dwelling plantation and also all of the tobacco due me from this Province for serving as an Assemblyman or otherwise and all of the tobacco due me in Queen Ann's County for serving as a Justice of the Peace. Wit: William Cowman.
Thomas Hammond to his Excellency, Samuel Ogle, Governor of Maryland: his petition asking for payment of tobacco due him to be made to Charles Browne.

047. 9 October 1751 - 17 October 1751 Sophia Emory to Sarah Emory, her mother - a gift of love - one negro woman named "Nann;" a negro boy named "William" and a negro boy named "Booder." Acknowledged before John Downes and John Downes, Jr.

048. 30 September 1751 - 24 October 1751 John Williams, Planter, to Nathaniel Wright, Planter - consideration ₤35 current - 100 acres, part of "Salsbury" - lying on the southwest branch of Coursica Creek - adjoining Williams' millpond. John Williams, Mary his wife, and Tabitha Nevitt acknowledged before William Hopper and Nathan Wright (the said Mary being first privately examined out of hearing of her husband). Alienation fine, four shillings sterling.

049. 26 October 1751 - 4 November 1751 John Allen Woodall, Planter, to John Harris and Thomas Sands - Power of Attorney to collect his accounts due and to pay to Cornelius Comegys' estate due to his children a balance of ₤84.8.4.½. Wit: William Hopper, John Williams.

050. John A. Woodell, for the consideration of securing payment to the estate of Cornelius Comegys for his children, by John Harris and Thomas Sands, a balance of ₤84.8.4.½; and according to Comegys' will the sum of ₤17.3.8.½ to his son John Comegys and the same to his second son Giasbartus Comegys and his daughter Jane Comegys; also a legacy of ₤30 to the child his widow was bigg with at the time of his death and also upon settling of one-fifth part of the share of Mary who dyed in her minority, which the shole makes ₤84.8.4.½ - conveyed to John Harris and Thomas Sands, all the goods and chattels that he ever was possessed with - it being the residue of the said Cornelius Comegys' estate. Wit: Vins. Benton, James

050. Burke.

051. 12 November 1751 Richard Hynson, Planter, to Turbutt Bettin, Planter - consideration 10,000 pounds of tobacco - 66 acres of land, part of "Wilkinson's Addition" and part of "Waltham." The dower of Susanna Mansfield, wife of William Mansfield, not warranted. Wit: Henry Johnson, Richard Tilghman. Richard and Ann his wife (she being first privately examined) acknowledged before Richard Tilghman, Justice of the Provincial Court. Alienation fine, one shilling, four pence sterling, paid to Richard Tilghman.

052. 21 November 1751 - 24 November 1751 John Willson, Jr., Planter, and Anne his wife; James Williams Nabb and Elizabeth his wife to David Harrington, Planter - consideration ₤25 - 55 acres, part of "Jones's Forrest" - lying on the north side of Muddy Branch of Choptank River just below the plantation where John Teat formerly lived. Acknowledged before John Downes and John Downes, Jr. Alienation fine, two shillings, two pence, half penny sterling.

053. 22 July 1751 - 27 November 1751 John Flynn, Laborer, and Rachel his wife of Kent County, Maryland, to John Nemo of Kent County, Maryland - Innkeeper - consideration ₤12 current money - one-fifth of the land called "Outrange," containing 200 acres lying in Queen Ann's County; formerly in the possession of Robert Green, then owner of the said lott. Wit: Jarves Spencer, Daniel Bryan. Flynn's receipt to Nemo was witnessed by S. Wilmer. Kent County: 23 July 1751 John Flynn and Rachel his wife acknowledged before Jarves Spencer and S. Wilmer - certified by James Smith, Clerk of Kent County, Maryland.

055. 21 November 1751 - 27 November 1751 John Willson, Jr., Planter, and Anne his wife; James Williams Nabb and Elizabeth his wife, to Philemon Green - consideration ₤25 current money - 45 acres, part of "Jones's Forrest" - lying on the south side of Muddy Branch of Choptank River below John Teat's plantation. Acknowledged before John Downes and John Downes, Jr. (the said Anne and Elizabeth being first privately examined out of hearing of their husbands). Alienation fine, one shilling, nine pence, half penny sterling, paid to Richard Tilghman.

056. 4 December 1751 - 5 December 1751 Thomas Butler, Planter, to Charles Browne, Merchant - consideration 7,400 pounds of tobacco - 100 acres, part of "Aulder Branch" - lying on the north side of Coursica Creek in Chester River, on the Aulder Branch. Thomas and Sarah his wife (she being first privately examined) acknowledged before Nathan Wright and N. Wright. Alienation fine, four shillings sterling.

058. 5 December 1751 Thomas Wilkinson and Thomas Caradine, appointed and qualified by William Hopper to value eighty acres of land under an old fence, with one old dwelling house, 20 feet, with two plank floors; one old logg'd kitchen, 20 feet by 16 feet; one logg'd cornhouse, 16 feet by 8 feet; an 8 feet square milk house, all old and in want of repairing; one 40-feet tobacco house in good repair, all but

058. the doors; about sixty apple trees, most of them small; some cherry trees and about fifty acres of woodland; the right of Henry Williams, a minor under the care of Rebecca Williams, his guardian. Annual value, 500 pounds of tobacco exclusive of the widow's thirds and the quitrents; the guardian permitted to get timber for repairs and fencing. 25 September 1751.

058. 4 December 1751 - 5 December 1751 John Browne, Schoolmaster, to Charles Browne , Merchant - consideration ₤90.2.9 current paper money - a negro girl slave named "Phillis;" one cow; two yearlings; one mare and colt named "Jewell;" one mare and colt named "Pyde;" one horse named "Cromwell;" one horse named "Steven." A chattel mortgage due on or before 4 December next. Acknowledged before James Brown and N. Wright.

059. 1 December 1751 - 16 December 1751 Charles McCarty brought before me a sorrell horse, taken up as a stray; middle sized and about ten years old. The owner proving his property and paying the costs can take him away. Charles Downes.

059. 2 January 1752 - 7 January 1752 Dowdall Thompson brought before me a stray horse, brown in colour, with hanging main (sic!) and pretty long tail. James Brown.

059. 9 Janaury 1752 - James Ponder of New Castle County, Province of Pennsylvania, Farmer, to Solomon Seney, Planter - consideration ₤80 current money - 112½ acres, part of "Clouds' Adventure" - lying on the south side of Hambleton's Branch, Chester River. James and Mary his wife (she being first privately examined out of his hearing) acknowledged before James Brown and John Seegar. Alienation fine, four shillings, six pence sterling, paid to Richard Tilghman.
19 December 1751.

061. 2 December 1751 - 9 January 1752 Christopher Green and Ann his wife, of Kent County upon Delaware, Planter, to John Vanderford, Planter - consideration 1,500 pounds of tobacco and ₤8 current money - 100 acres, part of "Christopher's Hazard" - lying on the south side of Hawknest Branch and on the west side of the head of Choptank River Branch. Christopher and Ann (she being first privately examined) acknowledged before John Downes and Jonathon Nicols.

062. 21 November 1751 - 20 January 1752 James Williams Nabb, Planter, and Elizabeth his wife, John Willson, Planter, and Anne his wife, to Charles Downes, Gentleman - consideration ₤87 current money - 87 acres, part of a tract of land at the head of Read's Creek, originally called "Jones's Addition" and upon resurvey thereof called "Wrenches Adventure" - lying on the south side of the main road that leads from Nathan Samuel Turbutt Wright's dwelling plantation to the main county road leading by the free school - adjoining Charles Downes' land, Thomas Hynson's land and "Jones's Hall," now possessed by John Willson. Acknowledged before John Downes and John Downes, Jr. (the said Elizabeth and Anne being first privately examined out of hearing

062. of their husbands). Alienation fine, three shillings, six pence sterling, paid to Richard Tilghman.

064. 28 January 1752 - 6 February 1752 Thomas Cox, Planter, to Jonathon Nicols - consideration £18 current money and 700 pounds of tobacco - all of the tobacco in my tobacco house; one bay mare called "Handsome;" one sow with six piggs; three shoats; one cow; one heifer, about three years old; one yearling heifer and the wheat now growing on the plantation whereon I now live. Acknowledged before John Downes.

065. 2 February 1752 - 6 Febraury 1752 William Bishop to Matthew Dockery - consideration £150 current money - 200 acres called "Dangerfield" - lying on the Southeast Branch, Chester River, near Hambleton's Branch. Acknowledged before William Hopper and Nathan Wright. Alienation fine, eight shillings sterling, paid to Richard Tilghman.

066. 20 February 1752 William Winchester Mason brought before me a small iron gray horse, a stray; about twelve hands high, four years old. The owner paying charges and proving his property may get him from the said Mason, living near the Nine Bridges of Tuckahoe Branch. N. Wright.

066. 20 February 1752 Nicholas Clouds of Kent Island, Innholder, to Thomas Marsh, Gentleman - consideration £80 current money - 200 acres called "Clouds' Choice" in Andover Branch, Chester River. Wit: Mary Carter, Richard Tilghman. Nicholas and Ruth his wife (she being first privately examined) acknowledged before Richard Tilghman, a Justice of the Provincial Court. Alienation fine, eight shillings sterling.

067. 3 March 1752 - 24 March 1752 Gideon Swift, Planter, to Thomas Sands, Planter - consideration 2,517 pounds of tobacco - 48 acres, part of "Northumberland," formerly laid out for Thomas Bostick - lying between Red Lyon and Unicorne Branches - adjoining Thomas Bostick's plantation. Acknowledged before James Brown and John Seegar. Alienation fine, one shilling, eleven pence sterling.

069. 24 May 1752 Samuel Blunt and John Granger, qualified and sworn before Joseph Sudler, to view and value the land of John Carter, son of John Carter, deceased, his guardian William Price - on 18 December last, entered upon the land and found one dwelling house, 36 feet long, 18 feet wide, with brick gable ends, plank floors above and below, wanting some small repairs; one old citchin (sic!), 30 feet by 15 feet, very much out of repair; logg quarter, 16 feet square; one corn house 16 by 6 feet; a small milk house, 8 by 6 feet; two tobacco houses, 30 feet by 20 feet each, wanting repair; one old dwelling house, 20 feet by 16 feet; one old logg house, 20 feet by 15 feet, the loggs not hewed; fifty-five old apple trees; twenty-eight young apple trees that bairs (sic!); the plantation in tolerable good repair of fencing; Price has the liberty to clear from a marked oak standing by a Bridge called Carter's Bridge and down with the main

069. to Jacob Carter's land. The annual rent, ₤9.10.0 current money. At a plantation called the "Ridge," one dwelling house 25 feet by 15 feet; one corn house, 12 feet long; one tobacco house, 40 feet by 20 feet; one tobacco house, 30 feet by 20 feet; a small nursery and about 30 acres of cleared ground in tolerable good fence. Price to have liberty to clear thirty acres more. Annual value, ₤3 current money.

069. 8 January 1752 - 24 March 1752 Edward Brown, Jr. and Charles Connor, qualified by Joseph Sudler to view and value the third part of a plantation called "Sillin" on Kent Island - belonging to Elizabeth Evans, a minor; Benjamin Kirby, her guardian - on 21 December last entered upon the land and found one dwelling house, 24 feet long, 16 feet wide with a shed adjoining, 24 feet by 12 feet, very much out of repair; one kitchen, 16 feet by 12 feet; one tobacco house, 40 feet by 38 feet; one logg corn house, not worth repairing; one logg house, out of repair; one tobacco house, 30 feet by 22 feet; one logg corn house, not worth repairing; one old gum logg house, good for little; 1,386 pannells of fencing; 46 sorry apple trees; annual value 500 pounds of tobacco; the guardian to get timber for necessary repairs.

070. 25 March 1752 Simon Keld to Grundy Pemberton - consideration ₤20 current money - 52 acres of land, part of "Keld's Inheritance" - lying on the north side of the road dividing Talbot and Queen Ann's County. Acknowledged before William Hopper and John Downes. Alienation fine, two shillings, one pence sterling, paid to Richard Tilghman.

071. 24 February 1752 - 25 March 1752 Violet Primrose, Innholder, to Thomas Marsh, Gentleman - consideration 5,500 pounds of tobacco - 100 acres of land, part of "Poplar Hill," bought by John Bath from Thomas Ubanks. Wit: Richard Tilghman, James Moffatt. Acknowledged before Richard Tilghman, Justice of the Provincial Court. Alienation fine, two shillings sterling.

072. 25 March 1752 Thomas Hacket and William Campbell, Jr., appointed and qualified by James Brown to view and value the land of Arthur Holt now in the possession of Dowdle Thompson, his guardian - on 23 December 1751 entered into the land called "Holt's Castle Hill" - lying on the south side of the Southeast Branch of Chester River, and found one dwelling house, 30 feet long, 18 feet wide, brick chimneys and shead (sic!) along one side; one kitching (sic!) 20 feet long, 16 feet wide, brick chimney with a shead along one side; one barn, 62 by 22 feet; three houses, 15 feet long, 12 feet wide; two houses, 10 feet square; one pidgen (sic!) house, 8 feet square; one small house, 6 by 4 feet; one old corn house, 20 by 9 feet - all covered with featheredged shingles; one logg'd house, 15 feet long, 12 feet wide, covered with clapboards; also 75 apple trees; the fencing in very bad repair; three acres of land to clear per year and timber to cut for necessary repairs; the annual value, 750 pounds of tobacco. Also the lands on the north side of the Southeast Branch

072. called "Price's Hill" belong to Arthur Holt and there was found one dwelling house 16 feet square, shingled ruff; one old logg'd house, 15 feet by 12 feet; one old logg'd corn house, 16 feet by 8 feet, very much out of repair; one tobacco house. 40 feet by 20 feet, shingled ruff (sic!); four apple trees; the fencing in middling repair; 3½ acres to clear per annum. Value, 800 pounds of tobacco, yearly.

073. 26 March 1752 Mary Elliott, Widow, to her son, Joseph Elliott - in consideration of her love and affection - 200 acres of land called "Clouds' Hermitage" - between the Beaver Dam Marsh and the Long Marsh. Acknowledged before William Hopper and N. Wright. Alienation fine, eight shillings sterling, paid to Richard Tilghman.

074. 27 March 1752 Joseph Elliott and Benjamin Roberts, appointed and sworn before John Seegar to view and value the lands of Benjamin Wells, a minor under the care of George Wells - on 3 January 1752 entered upon the land, 80 acres, called "Caleb's Lott," and found one logg dwelling house, 20 feet long, 16 feet wide, the loggs hewed, covered with 5 feet boards; one very old logg dwelling house, 20 feet long, 15 feet wide, round loggs, covered with 5 feet boards; one old tobacco house, 30 feet long, 20 feet wide, whole frame, covered with 5 feet boards; one old corn house, 15 feet long, 6 feet wide, covered with 5 feet boards; one hen house, 10 feet long, 5 feet wide, very old; 65 apple trees; 15 cherry trees; 4 Peach trees; 40 acres of cultivated land under a midling fence - annual value, 550 pounds of tobacco clear of quitrents. The guardian permitted to clear two acres annually and get timber for necessary repairs.

074. 27 March 1752 Benjamin Roberts and William Newnam, qualified by John Seegar to make a just estimate of the lands belonging to Humphrey Wells, a minor, George Wells, his guardian - on 13 December 1752 entered and found one-half acre of land with one warehouse, known as "Wells' Warehouse," 40 feet long, 24 feet wide with a ten feet shead (sic!) to the front and six prises (sic!) - the annual value, ₤3.10.0 current money of the Province.

075. 16 September 1751 Henry Rochester and Gideon Swift, qualified by John Seegar to make a just estimate of the lands belonging to Humphrey Wells, a minor, George Wells, his guardian - entered upon the land, 50 acres called "Crump's Fancy" and found two old logg'd dwelling houses; three apple trees; 18 old cherry trees; 28 acres of cleared ground under a mean fence - annual value, 100 pounds of tobacco and the quitrents - guardian permitted to get timber for repairs.

075. 13 December 1751 Benjamin Roberts and William Newnam, appointed to view and value the lands of John Wells, a minor, under the care of George Wells; 199½ acres called "Pearce's Land," entered and found one old frame dwelling house, 30 feet long, brick chimneys with two fireplaces; a citching (sic!) joyning to the dwelling house of 20 feet in length; one old milk house, 10 feet in length; one out dwel-

075. ling house for the overseer with round loggs, covered with ruff (sic!) boards, 15 feet long; 65 apple trees; 22 cherry trees; 75 acres of cultivated land under a mean fence - annual value, 300 pounds of tobacco - the guardian to clear two acres annually and get timber for necessary repairs.

076. 23 March 1752 - 28 March 1752 Sarah Hayes, Widow, to John Wallace of Chester Town, Merchant - consideration ₺43 current money - mortgages a negro man slave named "Charles." Wit: J. Bolton, John Downes.

076. 31 March 1752 Nathan Wright, Jr. and Henry Wrench, qualified by William Hopper to make just estimate of the land called "Upper Deal," the right of Elizabeth Evans, a minor, her guardian Benjamin Kirby - on 18 December last entered upon the plantation occupied by Alice Wright and found one clapboard dwelling house, 20 feet long, 15 feet wide; one tobacco house, 40 feet long, 20 feet wide, all wanting repair; a small orchard; the fencing in good repair; the guardian to clear five acres annually. On the plantation where Walter Edwards dwells, two dwelling houses, one 25 feet long, 22 feet wide; the other, 16 feet long, 12 feet wide; a tobacco house, 40 feet long, 20 feet wide; a cornhouse, old; all wanting repair; the fencing in good repair; the guardian to clear five acres and cut timber for repairs.

077. 3 April 1752 James Hobbs, Planter, to John Swift, Planter - consideration ₺20 current money - 50 acres of land in the Forrest of Choptank called "Bear's Harbour" - lying near a new mark't path from William Swift's to the head of Long Marsh. Wit: Richard Tilghman, Henry Johnson. James and Jane his wife (she being first privately examined) acknowledged before Richard Tilghman, Justice of the Provincial Court. Alienation fine, two shillings sterling, paid to Richard Tilghman.

078. 4 April 1752 - 9 April 1752 Margaret Kinninmont, Widow, to her daughter, Anne Kinninmont - a gift of love - a featherbed and furniture; a side saddle and all of her wearing apparell. Acknowledged before John Downes.

079. 27 March 1752 - 16 April 1752 Ambrose Kinninmont to William Elbert - consideration ₺100 current money - part of "Lambeth," willed to him by his father, John Kinninmont, 14 September 1748. Acknowledged before William Hopper and N. Wright. Alienation fine, four shillings sterling.

080. 3 July 1751 - 30 April 1752 Before Abraham Ogier, Notary Public in London (Eng.): William Anderson of London, Merchant, to Mr. Richard Lloyd of Maryland, Gentleman - Power of Attorney to conduct his affairs in this country. Witnessed by Benjamin Tasker, Jr. and James Henderson - sworn to, 14 February 1752 before George Steuart.

080. 4 May 1752 - 7 May 1752 William Carman to John Watson - consideration 1,200 pounds of tobacco and ₺5.10.0 current money of Maryland -

080. one servant man named John Hill. Witnessed by William Clayton and Ernal (sic!) Hawkins. Acknowledged before William Hopper.

081. 8 May 1752 John Seth brought before me a stray, white horse, middling size, about four years old. The owner proving his property and paying costs, may have him. John Downes.

081. 22 April 1752 - 21 May 1752 Thomas Bartlet, Planter, and Mary his wife, to David Register, Blacksmith - consideration ₤100 current - 120 acres, part of "Turner's Plains Addition" - given by Samuel Bartlet and Rachel his wife, 25 Janaury 1741 - adjoining "Edmondson's Green Close" and "Turner's Plains," laid out for Edward Turner - patented 18 September 1737 by Samuel Bartlet for 298 acres. Acknowledged before Nathan Wright and William Hopper. Alienation fine, four shillings, ten pence sterling, paid to Richard Tilghman.

082. 26 August 1749 - 1 June 1752 City and County of Bristol, England - At a Session of Gaol Delivery held 7 August instant, Sarah Phillips, Mary Burck, William Tully, John Collins and Thomas Lester, all convicted of felony were ordered to be transported to the Maryland colony for a term of seven years. Sig: William Cann, Town Clerk and Clerk of the Peace for the above City and County.

The following persons were imported into Maryland, in November 1749, by Messrs. Sedgly & Cheston, and consigned to and sold by me for their amount; John Collins who was said to be a surgeon was sold to Mr. John Tillotson for the term of seven years. Sig: Thomas Ringgold.

083. 2 June 1752 In the plantation of the subscriber is a small black horse, branded and has some white spots on the near side of his back. The owner may have him by proving his property and paying costs. Sig: John Davis (son of John).

083. 6 June 1752 John Davis, Jr. to John Primrose, Jr., his security in an action brought by Henry Jacobs - one old walnut desk; one chest; two old featherbeds; three tables; one small iron pot; one iron pott rack. Wit: John Brown, James Brown, Jr. Acknowledged before James Brown.

083. ADVERTISEMENT - 23 June 1752 At the plantation of Patrick Sexton at the head of Wei (sic!) River, a stray white horse, much flea bitten, short tail and about four feet high. The owner paying cost and proving his property may take him.

084. 16 May 1752 - 23 June 1752 John Hawkins and Sarah his wife, to Edward Brown, Sr. of Kent Island - consideration 10,000 pounds of tobacco and ₤25 current money of the Province - 107 acres, part of "Tully's Delight," on Island Creek near Ogletown. Acknowledged bebore William Hopper and John Seegar. Alienation fine, two shillings, two pence sterling, paid to Richard Tilghman.

085. 2 June 1752 - 23 June 1752 Thomas Nicolson, Planter, to John Seegar, Marrinor - consideration 3,000 pounds of tobacco - 39 acres of land, part of "Woodhouse;" also 11 acres of land, part of "Woodhouse Addition." Acknowledged before James Brown and Nathan Wright. Alienation fine, two shillings sterling, paid to Richard Tilghman.

087. 15 June 1752 - 23 June 1752 Ernault Hawkins and Jane his wife, to Edward Tilghman - consideration ₤20 paper currency and 6,000 pounds of tobacco - leases for twelve years, the plantation whereon they dwell, part of "Brampton," and a parcel adjoining called "Conquest," had of William Hopper. Wit: Richard Tilghman, John Hickes. Acknowledged before Richard Tilghman, Justice of the Provincial Court.

088. 2 July 1752 - 3 July 1752 Thomas Yoe brought a stray black horse before me, about thirteen and one-half hands high; a natural pacer and goeth fast and hard. The owner may claim by proving property and paying costs. N. Wright.

088. 4 June 1752 - 6 July 1752 William Thomas of Talbot County, Gentleman, and Elizabeth his wife, to Henry Fiddeman, Gentleman, consideration 6,000 pounds of tobacco - 10 acres of land, part of "Large Range," adjoining "Hacket's Garden" - heretofore sold by Thomas Fisher to Richard Fiddeman - also 55 acres, part of "Large Range" and part of "Hacket's Garden." Acknowledged before Robert Goldsborough and Tristram Thomas, Justices of the Peace for Talbot County; certified by John Leeds, Clerk of Talbot County. Alienation fine, two shillings, seven pence, half penny sterling.

090. 4 July 1752 - 6 July 1752 Absalom Sparks, Planter, and Elizabeth his wife; Robert Hawkins, Planter; John Sparks, Planter; Millington Sparks, Planter, and Caleb Sparks, Planter, to Edward Tilghman - consideration ₤107 current money - 100 acres, part of "Tully's Delight," on the Back Creek - also 100 acres, part of "Sparkes's Choice." Acknowledged before Richard Tilghman, Justice of the Provincial Court. Alienation fine, six shillings sterling.

091. 27 July 1752 - 28 July 1752 Thomas Baynard and John Casson, executors of John Baynard, deceased, to Peter Russum - a watermill and 20 acres of land on Dillavaughan's Branch - possessed by John Baynard under a 80-year lease from Samuel Ogle, Governor of Maryland - empowered to sell by John Baynard's will and in consideration of ₤292 current money, the mill and land, lying between Choptank River and Tuckahoe Creek. Acknowledged before John Downes and Jonathon Nicols. Alienation fine, ten pence sterling.

093. 28 July 1752 Edward Brown, Jr. and John Granger, qualified by Joseph Sudler to estimate the yearly value of "Beaver Neck" on Kent Island, for the minor, Reason Roles, his guardian, James Baxter - on 18 April 1752, entered upon the land and found one dwelling house, framed work, 24 by 18 feet, plank floor'd above and below, wants some repairs; one kitchin (sic!) 24 by 18 feet, out of repair; one framed dwelling house, 20 by 12 feet, out of repair; one logg corn house, 20 by 10

093. feet, framed; one tobacco house, 40 by 24 feet, wants repairing; one tobacco house, 30 by 22 feet, almost new; sixty old apple trees and 1,550 pannells of fencing. The annual rent, ₺14 paper currency. The guardian permitted to clear within the fence only, and to get timber for necessary repairs.

094. 28 July 1752 Nicholas Clouds and James Hutchings, qualified by Joseph Sudler to value "Pint Love" on Kent Island, the right of Anna Wickes, a minor, James Baxter, her guardian - on 18 April 1752, entered upon the land and found one dwelling house, 40 feet in length, with two brick gable ends, a brick seller, plank't above and below and in indifferent repair; one brick house adjoining to it, 20 feet by 18 feet, plank't floors above and below; one necessary house, old; one stable with new sawed loggs; one quarter; one tobacco house, 40 feet in length, indifferent repair; one tobacco house, 32 feet in length with a shead (sic!) and two prises, in indifferent repair; one good corn house; one old shed; one kitchin (sic!) with a stack of brick chimneys; one brick storehouse; one hen house; a garden with indifferent paling; the yard pails is indifferent; 22 old apple trees; 114 young thriving apple trees; one brick well; the fencing in indifferent repair. The annual value, ₺20 currency money; the guardian permitted to get timber for repairs but not to clear any ground for tobacco, corn, wheat or oats but what has been cleared already.

095. 28 July 1752 - 29 July 1752 Thomas Suell to Thomas Baggs - consideration 900 pounds of tobacco - two bay mares; one pide heifer; one pide steer. Wit: Mary Cox, Richard Harrington, Nathan Wright.

095. 29 July 1752 Sarah Emory, Widow, to John Bracco, Gentleman - 100 acres of land, part of "Hawkins' Pharsalia" - the residue of 200 acres left by John King, father of the said Sarah Emory to her, unconveyed by William Emory, deceased, and the said Sarah to John Emory. Mention made to a Writ of Entry obtained against her in April last. Wit: John Mayne, J. Wilkinson. Acknowledged before Richard Tilghman, Justice of the Provincial Court.

096. 28 May 1752 - 29 July 1752 Jeremiah Grasingham and Frances his wife of Talbot County, to Robert Goldsborough of Talbot, Gentleman - consideration ₺60 current money - 200 acres of land on the south side of Red Lyon Branch, being one third, given to the said Frances by her father, John Davis. Acknowledged before John Downes, and John Downes, Jr.

097. 4 June 1752 - 29 July 1752 Gideon Swift to Joseph Elliott - consideration 240 pounds of tobacco and ten shillings, six pence current money - 53 acres, part of "Lowe's Desire" - lying on the east side of Red Lyon Branch - adjoining part owned by Phillip Coppidge. Acknowledged before James Brown and John Seegar.

099. 30 July 1752 Received from Waitman Sipple the sum of ₺3.15.10 for alienation fine. Sig: Richard Tilghman.

099. 30 July 1752 - 31 July 1752 Samuel Hunter, Planter, to Thomas Baggs - consideration 30 shillings current money of the Province - 50 acres of land called "Hunter's Hope" - lying near "Lowe's Marsh." 30 July 1752 Joseph Hunter to Thomas Baggs - receipt of 30 shillings for the acknowledgment of the within deed, formerly being sold by my father, Joseph Hunter. Acknowledged by Samuel Hunter before James Brown and N. Wright. Alienation fine, two shillings sterling, paid to Richard Tilghman.

100. 29 Juny 1752 - 1 August 1752 Peter Johnson to Richard Warner - consideration 2,000 pounds of tobacco - 60 acres, part of "Albet's Desire" - lying on the west side of little Red Lyon Branch. Peter and Mary his wife (she being first privately examined out of hearing of her husband) acknowledged before N. Wright and John Downes. Alienation fine, two shillings, five pence sterling.

102. 3 April 1752 - 27 August 1752 John Willson, Planter, to Charles Nicols - consideration ₤170 current money - part of "Sayer's Addition" and part of "Branfield," both in possession of Benjamin Ainsworth, Joiner; also 50 acres, part of "Branfield," adjoining - in all, 250 acres lying in the freshes of Choptank River. Acknowledged before N. Wright and John Downes. Alienation fine, ten shillings sterling.

103. 17 June 1752 - 28 August 1752 William Hedges of Cecill County, Merchant, and Rebecca his wife, lately Rebecca Heath, executor of the will of James Paul Heath, late of Cecill County, Merchant, to John Ruth, Carpenter - consideration 20,580 pounds of tobacco - 50 acres, the remaining part of "Crumpton" - adjoining "Crump's Chance" - 150 acres adjoining, part of "Upper Heathworth;" also 143 acres, part of "Upper Heathworth." Acknowledged before D. Bayard and Adam Vanbebber, certified by Matthais Bordley, Clerk of Cecil County Court. Alienation fine, thirteen shillings, nine pence sterling.

105. 18 May 1752 - 28 August 1752 Richard Ragan of Talbot County, Joyner, and Lydia his wife, to Hawkins Downes, Planter - consideration 3,000 pounds of tobacco and ₤5 current money - 50 acres, part of "Millford" - mentions a division tree between George Golt and John Leonard, now between Risdon Bozman and Hawkins Downes. Acknowledged before Jonathon Nicols and John Downes. Alienation fine, two shillings sterling, paid to Richard Tilghman.

106. 25 August 1752 Samuel Roe and John Roe, qualified by N. Wright, to value the land of Thomas Chaires, a minor, George Smith, his guardian - on 18 August instant, entered upon the land and on the plantation occupied by Thomas Yoe, part of "Confusion" and part of "Smith's Forrest," found one frame dwelling house 24 feet long, 18 feet wide, in middling good repair; one logg house, 20 feet long, 16 feet wide, middling good; one barn, 40 feet long, 22 feet wide, middling good; one old logg corn house; one old out framed house not worth repairing; a good young orchard and other scattering fruit trees; fence in middling good repair; the guardian permitted to clear fifteen acres; annual value, 600 pounds of tobacco.

107. 21 August 1752 - 28 August 1752 William Harrington, Planter, and Elizabeth his wife, to Robert Brodey, Taylor - consideration ₺26 current money - 50 acres of land, part of "Henry's Lott" - lying on the east side of a path that leads to John Culbreath's. Acknowledged before William Hopper and Nathan Wright. Alienation fine, two shillings sterling, paid to Richard Tilghman.

109. 16 September 1752 John Ruth, Carpenter, to John Walters, Planter - consideration 8,580 pounds of tobacco - 143 acres, part of "Upper Heathworth" - adjoining "Crump's Chance." Acknowledged before William Hopper and Nathan Wright. Alienation fine, five shillings, nine pence sterling.

110. 16 September 1752 John Ruth, Carpenter, to Samuel McCosh, Planter - consideration 18,000 pounds of tobacco, 150 acres, part of "Upper Heathworth" on Island Creek - 50 acres, part of "Crumpton," adjoining "Crump's Chance." Acknowledged before William Hopper and Nathan Wright. Alienation fine, eight shillings sterling.

112. 14 April 1752 - 18 September 1752 James Hamilton, Planter, to Theophilus Randall of Kent County, Maryland, Planter - consideration ₺75 current money and 8,500 pounds of tobacco - 227 acres of land on Double Creek, called "Baron Neck" - adjoining a parcel laid out for Richard Tilghman, between Double and Hawkins' Creeks; also 50 acres called "James' Lott" - adjoining, and lying between Double and Hambleton's Creeks. James and Anne his wife (she being first privately examined out of his hearing) acknowledged before William Hopper and Nathan Wright. Alienation fine, eleven shillings, one penny sterling.

114. 29 July 1752 - 19 October 1952 Jeremiah Jadwin, Planter, to Robert Sumpter - release of a mortgage made 24 August 1749 on "Watery Plaine" at the head of the Maple Swamp, in the woods between the head of Choptank River and the Long Marsh. Acknowledged before Jonathon Nicols and John Downes.

115. 29 July 1752 - 19 October 1752 Robert Sumpter to Charles Browne, Merchant - consideration 1,500 pounds of tobacco - 50 acres called "Watery Plaine." Acknowledged before Jonathon Nicols and John Downes. Alienation fine, two shillings sterling.

116. 18 October 1752 - 19 October 1752 Thomas Butler brought before me a stray horse, a bay gelding - the owner unknown. Nathan Wright.

116. 25 October 1752 Nathaniel Connor brought before me a sorrel horse about 13 hands high - the owner proving his property and paying costs, can have him. John Downes.

117. 23 October 1752 - 1 November 1752 William Hedges of Cecil County, Merchant, and Rebecca his wife, lately Rebecca Heath, executrix of James Paul Heath, to John Ruth - consideration 20,580 pounds of tobacco - 50 acres, the remains of "Crumpton;" 150 acres, part of

117. "Upper Heathworth;" and 143 acres, another part of "Upper Heathworth." Wit: Richard Tilghman, E. P. Wilmer. Acknowledged before Richard Tilghman, Justice of the Provincial Court.

119. 7 October 1752 - 2 November 1752 John Offley Collins, Planter, to John Smyth, Chirurgeon - consideration ₤50 paper currency and 2,500 pounds of tobacco - 75 acres, part of "Spread Eagle," on the Southeast Branch of Chester River, on the south side of Collins' millpond - adjoining a former purchase by John Smyth. Acknowledged before James Brown and Nathan Wright. Alienation fine, one shilling, six pence sterling.

120. 18 September 1752 - 2 November 1752 Thomas Richardson Roe to George Baynard - consideration ₤82 current money and 300 pounds of tobacco - 100 acres called "Roe's Chance" - lying in Tully's Neck. Acknowledged before William Hopper and Nathan Wright. Alienation fine, four shillings sterling.

121. 16 November 1752 - 28 November 1752 James Brown, Edward Brown and Thomas Richardson Roe, appointed to make a just estimate of the value of the lands of William Elliott, a minor under the guardianship of William Austin - on 28 October last, entered into the plantation in the possession of William Austin, part of a tract that belonged to George Elliott and found one old logg dwelling house, 20 feet in length, not worth repairing; one old tobacco house, 30 feet long, not worth repairing; a middling good orchard of 90 apple trees and other scattering fruit trees; the fencing very much out of repair. The guardian allowed to clear twenty acres of land. Annual rent, 300 pounds of tobacco.

122. 27 October 1752 - 30 November 1752 Abraham Boon, Planter, and Rebecca his wife, to Anthony Cox, Planter - consideration 4,000 pounds of tobacco - 100 acres, "Cox'es Desire" - near Dickenson's Marsh. Abraham and Rebecca (she being first privately examined) acknowledged before Nathan Wright and N. Wright. Alienation fine, four shillings sterling, paid to Richard Tilghman.

123. 1 December 1725 John Bracco, Planter, to Charles Browne, Merchant - consideration 1,500 pounds of tobacco - 33½ acres, part of "Long Marsh Ridge Enlarged" - lying in the Forrest of Choptank near a great island in the Long Marsh adjoining "Burk's Expectation," "Hemsley's Discovery" and "Hogg Harbour." Acknowledged before Richard Tilghman, Justice of the Provincial Court. Alienation fine, one shilling, four pence sterling.

124. 28 November 1752 - 1 December 1752 John Breerely, Planter, of Talbot County, and Isabell his wife, to William Lambdin of Talbot County, Planter - consideration ₤60 current money - a parcel of land bequeathed to him by his grandmother, Mary Wrightson, lying on the Unicorn Branch - called "Reviving Springs." Acknowledged before Risdon Bozman and Matthew Tilghman, Justices of the Peace for Talbot County and certified by John Leeds, Clerk of Talbot County Court. Alienation fine, six shillings, eight pence, half penny sterling.

125. 19 October 1752 - 1 December 1752 Sarah Emory, Widow, to Thomas Lee, Gentleman - consideration 12,000 pounds of tobacco - 100 acres of land in Tully's Neck, called "Hawkins' Pharsalia" - the residue of 200 acres left by John King to the said Sarah, unconveyed by William Emory, deceased and the said Sarah to John Emory. Wit: Nathan Samuel Turbutt Wright, Charles Downes. Acknowledged before Richard Tilghman, Justice of the Provincial Court. Alienation fine, four shillings sterling.

127. 6 December 1752 Henry Lizenbee to Gideon Swift - consideration 4,500 pounds of tobacco - 150 acres, called "Lowther's Chance" - lying in the borders of Queen Ann's County. Acknowledged before William Hopper and John Seegar. Alienation fine, six shillings sterling, paid to Richard Tilghman.

128. 12 January 1753 James Seth, City of Philadelphia, Ship Joyner, to Charles Seth, Yoeman - consideration ₤116 lawful money - 100 acres, his part of "Mt. Mill," "Addition," and "Bennett's Outlet" - 400 acres near the head of Back Wye - willed by Charles Seth, 23 August 1737 to his four sons, i.e. John, James, Charles and Jacob Seth, to be divided between them. Wit: Richard Tilghman, Dennis Carey. James and Anne his wife (she being first privately examined out of hearing of her husband) acknowledged before Richard Tilghman, Justice of the Provincial Court. Alienation fine, four shillings sterling.

130. 20 January 1753 Henry Jacobs, Planter, and Anne his wife, to Anthony McCulloch, Merchant - consideration ₤45 current money - the old prison standing in Queens Town and one-fourth acre of land whereon the prison stands - on Courthouse Street. Acknowledged before Richard Tilghman, Justice of the Provincial Court.

131. 30 July 1752 - 24 January 1753 Samuel Massey, Innholder, to Edward Lloyd, Esquire - consideration ₤240.3.1 current money - 300 acres of land near Kings Town, Chester River, called and known as "Chestnut Neck" - conveyed by John Hamer and Sarah his wife, to William Dames and by Dames to Samuel Massey. Acknowledged before James Brown and Nathan Wright. Alienation fine, twelve shillings sterling.

132. 25 January 1753 Edward Neale, Gentleman, and Elizabeth his wife, to Edward Tilghman - consideration ₤214 sterling - 200 acres of land called "Discovery" - adjoining "Collington" - also part of "Tully's Delight," purchased by Elizabeth Neale from Ernault Hawkins and devised to Hawkins by his grandfather, James Hawkins about 23 April 1717. Wit: Richard Tilghman, Anthony McCulloch. Edward and Elizabeth (she being first privately examined out of his hearing) acknowedged before Richard Tilghman, Justice of the Provincial Court. Alienation fine, twelve shillings sterling.

134. 23 January 1753 - 25 January 1753 Edward Brown, Planter, to James Hollyday, Gentleman - consideration ₤268 current money of the Province - 134 acres of land, part of "Macklinborough" - adjoining a part sold by John Hawkins and Sarah his wife to Hollyday, 4 February 1734.

134. The land lies on the road leading from Ogletown down the county and on a branch of Dividing Creek. Acknowledged before James Brown and Nathan Wright. Alienation fine, four shillings, one penny sterling, paid to Richard Tilghman.

136. 28 January 1753 On the 24th instant, James Tuite brought before me a black mare, trespassing on him as a stray - the owner proving his property and paying costs can take her away. John Downes.

136. 8 August 1752 - 2 February 1753 William Cole of Talbot County, Wheelwright, to Edward Lloyd, Esquire - consideration 43,070 pounds of tobacco - part of "Hemsley's Park" and part of "Hemsley's Brittania" - chiefly in Talbot County on the south side of the county road leading from Wye Mill to Tuckahoe Bridge - adjoining "Costin's Chance," part of "Hemsley's Brittania," the lands of Ferdinando Callahane, "Boston" and "Noble's Meadows," in all, 300 acres. Also part of the land called "Hilsdon" and part of "Costin's Chance," in Talbot County, conveyed by Samuel Cockayne and Anne Cockayne late of Talbot County, deceased, to William Cole - the deed recorded in Talbot County. Wit: John Emory, Will. Geddes. Acknowledged in Talbot County before Robert Hall and John Goldsborough, Justices of the Peace, certified by John Leeds, Clerk of the Court. Alienation fine, seventeen shillings, five pence, three farthings sterling, paid to John Bozman, Receiver.

138. 10 November 1752 - 9 February 1753 Thomas Nicholson, Planter, to John Holding, Planter - consideration 4,000 pounds of tobacco and ₤10 current Maryland money - 50 acres, "Nicholson's Fancy" on the head of Unicorn Branch - adjoining "Woodhouse" - another parcel of "Woodhouse," 50 acres and another parcel of 14 acres, part of "Woodhouse Addition." Acknowledged before William Hopper and Nathan Wright. Alienation fine, four shillings, seven pence sterling.

139. 5 February 1753 - 9 February 1753 Thomas Price, Planter, to Christopher Cross Routh, Planter - consideration 18,000 pounds of tobacco - 100 acres, part of "Chestnut Meadow" - also part of "Conclusion," adjoining, _?_ acres. Acknowledged before N. Wright and Nathan Wright. Alienation fine, seven shillings, seven pence, half penny sterling.

140. 10 February 1753 Francis Bright, Planter, and Ann his wife, to Benjamin Kirby, Gentleman - consideration ₤25 current - 50 acres called "Cooper's Quarter" - lying on Kent Island at the head of Howell's Branch. Wit: Richard Tilghman, Alexander Williamson, Jr. Acknowledged before Richard Tilghman, Justice of the Provincial Court. Alienation fine, two shillings sterling.

141. 28 August 1752 - 22 February 1753 William Greenwood to Edward Clayton - consideration ₤205.2.6 current money of Maryland - 113 acres, "Broad Neck," on Wye River. Acknowledged before William Hopper and Nathan Wright. Alienation fine, four shillings, six pence, half penny sterling.

144. 8 February 1753 - 22 February 1753 Thomas Harris, Sheriff, to Thomas Willson - 720 acres, the land of William Greenwood, debtor to the estate of Richard Bennett, Edward Lloyd, executor - "Plaindealing" and "Jackson's Boggs." Wit: Thomas Browne, Robert Campbell. Acknowledged before Richard Tilghman, Justice of the Provincial Court. Alienation fine, ₤1.3.9½ sterling, paid to Richard Tilghman.

145. 9 February 1753 - 24 February 1753 Gideon Swift, Planter, to Bexley John Lambdin, Joyner - consideration ₤55 current money and 2,000 pounds of tobacco - 48 acres, part of "Swift's Outlet" - adjoining "Northumberland;" 52 acres, pt. of "Northumberland." Gideon and Ann his wife (she being first privately examined out of his hearing) acknowledged before James Brown and John Seegar. Alienation fine, four shillings sterling.

146. 16 December 1752 - 6 March 1753 Davenport Wells and Mary his wife, to John McClean - consideration 3,000 pounds of tobacco and ₤8 current- 50 acres on the Unicorn Branch in the Forrest of Queen Ann's, called "Wells' Chance." Acknowledged by Davenport and Mary (she being first privately examined) before James Brown and John Seegar. Alienation fine, two shillings sterling.

147. 21 December 1752 - 8 March 1753 Baldwin Kemp to Nathaniel Covington - consideration 7,000 pounds of tobacco - 91 acres of land called "Hinsely's Plaine" - lying in Tully's Neck - adjoining "Alcock's Pharsalia." Acknowledged before N. Wright and John Seegar. Alienation fine, three shillings, eight pence sterling.

148. 9 February 1753 - 27 March 1753 Charles Raley to Thomas Seward, Jr. - consideration ₤70 current money - 90 acres called "Hawkins' Range," on Beaver Dam Marsh. Acknowledged before James Brown and John Seegar. Alienation fine, three shillings, seven pence, half penny sterling, paid to Richard Tilghman.

150. 24 March 1753 - 27 March 1753 Bexley John Lambdin, Joyner, to William Bennett, Planter - consideration ₤50 current and 5,000 pounds of tobacco - 100 acres, "Lambden's Adventure" - on the southwest side of Red Lyon Branch. Acknowledged before Nathan Wright and John Seegar. Alienation fine, four shillings sterling.

153. 15 December 1753 - 28 March 1753 Thomas Dockery and Nathan Wright, Jr. qualified by William Hopper to view and value the lands and plantation belonging to Henry Williams, minor son of Abraham Williams - George Williams, his guardian - a tract of land called "Millford," 123 acres, 80 or 90 acres cleared, under a midling old fence; about 90 apple trees, most of them small; about 10 cherry and peach trees; one old dwelling house, out of repair, 20 feet long and 16 feet broad with two plank floors; one old kitchen of 20 feet in length and 16 feet in breadth; one old milk house; one corn house; one hen house; one good barn (only wants raising from the ground) of 40 feet by 20 feet. The guardian has liberty to cut timber and to clear 500 square yards of land yearly. Annual rent, 1,000 pounds of tobacco.

153. 17 March 1753 - 29 March 1753 John Willson to Henry Fiddeman, Gentleman - consideration £100 current money and 4,000 pounds of tobacco - 200 acres, part of "Branfield," originally surveyed for William Cross for 800 acres of land in the whole; which 200 acres is that part which John Willson, deceased, by his last will and testament bequeathed to his son Nathan Willson and by his death became the right of John, his brother. Acknowledged before Jonathon Nicols and John Downes. Alienation fine, eight shillings sterling, paid to Richard Tilghman.

154. 31 March 1753 Richard Blunt of Kent County, Delaware, Gentleman, to John Bracco, Planter - consideration 5,000 pounds of tobacco - 50 acres of land, called "Long Marsh Ridge" in the Forrest of Choptank and on a small drain of the Long Marsh. Acknowledged before Joseph Sudler and Nathan Wright. Alienation fine, two shillings sterling.

156. 31 March 1753 Alexander Toulson, Planter, to John Seegar, Planter - a partition of jointly held land called "Partnership" - lying in the fresh runs of Island Creek, 400 acres in the whole. Each to the other, 67 1/8 acres of the part divided. Acknowledged before Joseph Sudler and James Browne.

157. 14 February 1753 - 2 April 1753 Thomas Baily, Planter, to Mary Kemp and Rebecca Harris his daughters - in consideration of his love and affection - part of "Tom's Fancy Enlarged" - bought of Fairclough Wright. Wit: Edward Tucker, John Underwood, Thomas Wilkinson. Acknowledged before William Hopper and Nathan Wright. Alienation fine, six shillings sterling.

158. 5 April 1753 Charles Browne, Merchant, to David Register, Blacksmith - consideration 15,000 pounds of tobacco - 100 acres of land, part of "Bradburn's Delight" otherwise "Baily's Delight" (attached by Charles Browne & Company from Thomas Bailey, Jr.) - on a cove of Coursica Creek. Wit: Richard Tilghman, William Johnson. Charles and Priscilla his wife (she being first privately examined) acknowledged before Richard Tilghman, Justice of the Provincial Court. Alienation fine, four shillings sterling.

159. 7 April 1753 John Ruth, Carpenter, to John Walters, Planter - consideration 8,580 pounds of tobacco - 143 acres, part of "Upper Heathworth" - adjoining "Crump's Chance." Wit: Richard Tilghman, Macklin Elbert. Acknowledged before Richard Tilghman, Justice of the Provincial Court.

160. 12 April 1753 William Manning brought a sorrell horse before me, about four years old, trespassing on his enclosure - the owner paying costs and proving his property may take him away. John Downes.

160. 6 April 1753 - 12 April 1753 George Burroughs has taken up a stray small brown mare, about nine years old, twelve hands high - apply to George Burroughs, living in Queen Anne's Forrest - the owner proving

160. his property and paying costs may have her. John Seegar.

161. 21 April 1753 - 26 April 1753 John Nicolson brought a stray, bay mair (sic!) before me, seven or eight years old, twelve hands high. Apply to John Nicolson - the owner proving his property and paying costs may have her. John Seegar.

161. 19 April 1753 - 3 May 1753 Elizabeth Lambdin, Spinster, to Gideon Swift, Planter - consideration ₤30 current money - one negro boy named "Isaac." Wit: Thomas Stanton, Mary Ann Mayson, George Lambdin. Vincent Benton witnessed Elizabeth's receipt to Gideon Swift.

161. 3 April 1753 - 9 May 1753 John Seegar, Gentleman, to James Walters and Samuel Walters, Planters - consideration ₤125 current money - 150¼ acres, part of "Partnership" - in the fresh runs of Island Creek - also another part of "Partnership," containing 67 1/8 acres. John and Elizabeth his wife (she being first privately examined out of his hearing) acknowledged before James Brown and Nathan Wright. Alienation fine, eight shillings, nine pence sterling, paid to Richard Tilghman.

163. 27 April 1753 - 17 May 1753 William Clayton and Thomas Butler, Planters, to Joseph Sudler - consideration 16,000 pounds of tobacco - 200 acres, part of a tract of 400 acres on Red Lyon Branch, part of "Sheppard's Forrest" - formerly in Talbot County now in Queen Ann's. William and Sarah his wife; Thomas and Sarah his wife, acknowledged before William Hopper and Nathan Wright (the two wives being first privately examined out of hearing of their husbands). Alienation fine, eight shillings sterling.

165. 19 May 1753 Hynson Wright, Planter, late of Queen Ann's County but now of the Colony of North Carolina, to Christopher Cox, Gentleman - consideration ₤250 current money of the Province of Pensilvania - 300 acres, part of "Lowe's Arcadia" - lying on the west side of the Southeast Branch of Island Creek, now or heretofore called Elliott's Branch. Acknowledged before William Hopper and Nathan Wright. Alienation fine, twelve shillings sterling.

166. 31 May 1753 In my possession, a bright bay colt about three years old, taken up as a stray - the owner proving his property and paying costs, may take him away. Abraham Betton - 26 May 1753.

166. 30 January 1753 - 31 May 1753 Absalom Sparks and Elizabeth his wife, to Edward Brown - consideration ₤160 current - 124 acres of land, part of "Brampton" - adjoining "Reed's Mannor." Acknowledged before William Hopper and Nathan Wright (the said Elizabeth Sparks being first privately examined). Alienation fine, two shillings, six pence sterling.

168. 22 December 1753 - 8 June 1753 John Primrose, Planter, and Sarah his wife, to William Campbell, Planter - consideration ₤70 current money and 10,500 pounds of tobacco - 150 acres, part of "Hamilton's

168. Hermitage," formerly in Talbot County - on the north side of the Dividing Branch, Chester River - begins on a point near a place called the Cathole - adjoining "Price's Hill." Also 30 acres, part of a tract surveyed for and patented to John Primrose, uncle to the above grantor. Wit: Charles Brown, Robert Campbell. Acknowledged before Richard Tilghman, Justice of the Provincial Court. On 6 March 1753, Sarah, wife of John Primrose, acknowledged before James Brown and Nathan Wright, two Justices of the Peace for Queen Ann's County. Alienation fine, four shillings, three pence sterling.

170. 18 December 1752 - 18 June 1753 Daniel Hamer of Kent County, Province of Maryland, Taylor, and Anne his wife, daughter and heir at law of Robert Ivy, deceased, to John Wallace of Kent County (Md.), Merchant - consideration ŀ40 current - 100 acres of land called the "Triangle" - on the north side of Coursica Creek - granted 3 July 1682 to Robert Smith - adjoining the land laid out for George Pascall and the land of William Hemsley. Wit: Charles Scott, William Hynson, Justices of Kent County - James Smith, Clerk of Kent County. Alienation fine, four shillings sterling, paid to Richard Tilghman.

171. 20 March 1753 - 19 June 1753 James Scotten and Anne his wife, Planter and Spinster, to John Price, Cart wheelwright - consideration 12,000 pounds of tobacco - 50 acres , part of "Tom's Fancy Enlarged," lying in Tully's Neck - adjoining parts of the same sold to John Loyd and Nathaniel Read. Warranted against the heirs of Thomas Hynson Wright and Charles Lizenbe. Acknowledged before James Brown and John Seegar. Alienation fine, two shillings sterling.

172. 7 June 1753 - 19 June 1753 James Williams Nabb, Planter, to Hynson Downes - lease of "Wrench'es Farm" at the head of Wye Branches, from 10 December 1752 for a term of seven years - paying annually 600 pounds of tobacco and four shillings sterling. Nabb to find nails for repairs or building - Hynson Downes to sell or diapose of all dead timber, paying Nabb one-half of the profits; also give to Nabb one-half of the timber felled in clearing. Acknowledged before James Brown and Richard Costin.

174. 23 June 1753 - 28 June 1753 John Baker, Planter, to John Bracco, Planter - consideration 950 pounds of tobacco - one gray mare about eight years old and her colt, now about one year old - both lately bought of Martha Welsh. Wit: Nathan Baker, John Phillips. Acknowledged before William Hopper.

174. 26 June 1753 The Brigantine "Fancy," lying at anchor in Chester River, bound for Bristoll, takes in tobacco on freight at ŀ7 sterling per tonn consigned to Messrs. Williams, Allyne & Company, Merchants in Bristoll. Sig: Daniel Bird.

174. 27 June 1753 Thomas Elliott Hutchins brought before me a stray, an old bay mare and a young sorrel mare colt with a blaze in her face - the old mare has a sore back. Sig: Joseph Sudler.

174. 21 June 1753 - 16 July 1753 Peregrine Frisby of Cecil County, Province of Maryland, Gentleman, to Frances Willson, Mary Willson, Elizabeth Willson and Anne Willson, daughters of Robert Willson, deceased, late of Queen Ann's County - in consideration of two shillings - 264 acres of land on Kent Island known as "Crafford," for a term of one year - by virtue of the statute for transferring uses into possession. Wit: Jacob Jones, Charles Scott.

175. 22 June 1753 - 16 July 1753 Peregrine Frisby of Cecil County, Province of Maryland, Gentleman, to Frances Willson, Mary Willson, Elizabeth Willson and Anne Willson, daughters of Robert Willson, deceased, late of Queen Ann's County - in consideration of ₤336.15.0 current money - 264 acres on Kent Island called "Crafford." Peregrine and Ann his wife, acknowledged before Jacob Jones and Charles Scott, Justices of the Peace for Kent County - James Smith, Clerk of Kent County. Alienation fine, five shillings, three pence, half penny sterling, paid to Richard Tilghman.

177. 6 July 1753 - 16 July 1753 Sweatnam Burn, Mariner, to William Hopper, Gentleman - Power of Attorney to conduct his affairs. Wit: John Burk, James Hollyday. Acknowledged before Nathan Wright.

177. 15 June 1753 - 19 July 1753 William Rogers and Martha his wife, of Cecill County, Maryland, Taylor - the said Martha being co-heir with Elizabeth Bruer of St. Mary's County unto Agnes McKetrick, relict of Dr. Andrew McKetrick, deceased, of Kent County, Maryland - to Abraham Milton of Kent County, Planter - consideration ₤35.8.0 current - 75 acres of land, a moiety of 150 acres, part of "Crump's Forrest" - lying on the east side of the Southwest Branch of Island Creek. Wit: John Veazey, Thomas Savin, Justices of the Peace for Kent County - before whom William and Martha acknowledged (the said Martha being first privately examined). Matthew Bordley, Clerk of Kent County.

179. 20 July 1753 Mary Scotten to her children: Nathaniel Scotten, Catherine Scotten and Esther Scotten - a gift of love - to her son, Nathaniel, 43 acres known as "Nathaniel's Addition" - adjoining "Salsbury Plains" on Choptank River - if he should die before he reaches the age of twenty-one, the land is to go to my son Richard Scotten - to my daughter Catherine Scotten, at age eighteen or day of marriage, one featherbed and boulster; one rugg; one blankett and one sheet; and "Scotten's Outlet" - lying on the west side of the main branch of Choptank River opposite to the Horsehead Neck, 50 acres. If Catherine should die before reaching twenty-one or day of marriage, the gift is for my daughter Esther Scotten. Acknowledged before Nathan Wright and John Downes. Alienation fine, three shillings, nine pence sterling, paid to Richard Tilghman.

180. 21 July 1753 John Emory, Planter, to Thomas Emory, Jr., his son - in consideration of the love and affection borne to him - 187 acres of land called "Roberts' Range" and "Roberts' Range Addition," in the Horsehead Neck whereon the said Thomas now dwells. Wit: John Clemans, Richard Grason. Acknowledged before Richard Tilghman,

180. Justice of the Provincial Court. Alienation fine, seven shillings, six pence sterling, paid to Richard Tilghman.

181. 30 March 1753 - 2 August 1753 Thomas Marsh of Kent Island to John Smith, Surgion (sic!) - consideration 6,000 pounds of tobacco - a parcel of land called "Marye's Portion," lately lying in Kent County but now according to the late division of the counties, lying in Queen Ann's - near the middle of Kent Island and adjoining the land of Richard Blunt and Phillip Connyer - beginning at an oak tree by the road at the head of Tarkill Creek and running to the head of Martain's Creek - adjoining the land of Phillip Connyer called and known as "Broad Creek" and the Tarkill Field - 150 acres. Acknowledged before N. Wright and John Downes, Jr. Alienation fine, six shillings sterling, paid to Richard Tilghman.

183. 31 March 1753 - 16 August 1753 John Thomas, Elizabeth Thomas his wife, and Mary Rowland, all of Talbot County, to John Covington - consideration ₤100 current money of the Province - 254 acres called "Rowland's Hazard" - adjoining "Content," lying on Smith's Branch, and "Providence," formerly possessed by Charles Stevens - the part formerly possessed by Henry Covington. Acknowledged before Joseph Sudler and Nathan Wright (the said Elizabeth Thomas being first privately examined out of hearing of her husband). Alienation fine, ten shillings, three pence, half penny sterling.

184. ADVERTISEMENT. 16 August 1753 - 20 August 1753 At the plantation of James Nabb, neare the Free School, a stray, small black meare (sic!) with a white face - the owner may have her again by proving property and paying costs.

184. 3 August 1753 - 29 August 1753 Stephen Jarman and Elizabeth his wife, to George Baynard - consideration ₤200 current - 125 acres called "Hogg Harbour" - lying near the head of the northeastern main branch of Tuckahoe Creek and on the east side of the Long Marsh - the beginning tree at the head of a little swamp near the head of the Bee Tree Marsh. Acknowledged before N. Wright and Nathan Wright. Alienation fine, five shillings sterling.

186. 24 July 1753 - 31 August 1753 John Hadley to James Massey, Jr., Planter - consideration ₤20 current money and 1,000 pounds of tobacco - 30 acres, part of "Friendship" - adjoining a parcel sold by Thomas Hynson Wright to James Massey, Sr. Acknowledged before James Brown and John Seegar. Alienation fine, one shilling, two pence, half penny sterling.

187. 24 July 1753 - 31 August 1753 John Hadley to James Massey, Jr., Planter - consideration ₤40 current money and 2,000 pounds of tobacco - 50 acres, part of "Friendship." Acknowledged before James Brown and John Seegar. Alienation fine, two shillings sterling.

189. 25 August 1753 - 31 August 1753 Richard Wells, Sr., Gentleman, to Richard Wells, Jr. of Kent County, Delaware, Practitioner of Phy-

189. sick and son of Richard Wells, Sr. - a gift of all of his lands and tenements either in England, Ireland, Scotland or America and particularly all in Virginia, Maryland, or Pensilvania, or in the counties of Newcastle, Kent and Sussex on Delaware in America. Acknowledged before James Brown and John Seegar.

190. 22 June 1753 - 31 August 1753 Rebecca Harrington and George Harrington to Nathan Harrington - a gift of love - a parcel of land called "Beaver Dams Addition." Wit: John Newnam, Thomas Golt.

190. 28 August 1753 - 31 August 1753 John Davis and Christopher Cross Ruth, qualified by N. Wright to view and value the estate of Thomas Wright, a minor - called "Wright's Chance" - John Tillotson, his guardian. On 17th of August instant, entered unto a small parcel of cleared ground and found one logg house, 18 feet long, 16 feet wide, rough work; about 100 rails; four small cherry trees and one small apple tree - the guardian not to exceed more than eight acres in clearing per annum, with liberty of getting timber for necessary repairs. Rent, 200 pounds of tobacco yearly.

190. 30 August 1753 - 31 August 1753 John Primrose to Henry Lizenbe - consideration ₤8 current money - thirteen sheep; three cows; two heifers; one steer; one calf. Wit: William Benton, John Culbreath, Jr. Acknowledged before John Downes, Jr.

191. 6 March 1753 - 31 August 1753 Samuel Sparks to Valentine Thomas Honey - consideration ₤20 current money and 3,000 pounds of tobacco - 100 acres of land, part of "Mitchell's Adventure" - lying on the southeast side of Island Creek - adjoining "Tully's Delight." Acknowledged before James Brown and John Seegar. Alienation fine, four shillings sterling, paid to Richard Tilghman.

192. 2 August 1753 - 6 September 1753 William Mansfield, Planter, and Susanna his wife, to James Harvey of Kent Island - consideration ₤32.10.0 current - one-half of "Goldhawk's Enlargement" on Kent Island. Wit: Richard Tilghman, James Hollyday. Anthony McCulloch witnessed Harvey's receipt of payment. William and Susanna (she being first privately examined) acknowledged before Richard Tilghman, Justice of the Provincial Court.

194. 18 August 1753 - 6 September 1753 William Mountique, son of Abraham Mountique, Planter, to Thomas Baggs - consideration ₤5 current - one gray mare. Wit: James Silvester. Acknowledged before Jonathon Nicols.

194. 4 October 1753 Absalom Timm brought before me, taken up as a stray, a white stallion about eight years old and near thirteen hands high, the owner desiring to prove his property and pay charges, can take him away from Timm, living in Choptank Forrest. N. Wright.

194. 17 August 1753 - 8 October 1753 Nicholas Rakes and Mary his wife, to Stephen Jarman - consideration ₤20 current money and 2,000 pounds

194. of tobacco - a tract of land on the northwest side of the Frenchwoman's Branch called "Hoghole" (except the graveyard and twenty feet of ground about it). Nicholas and Mary (she being first privately examined out of his hearing) acknowledged before William Hopper and Nathan Wright.

195. 13 August 1753 - 18 October 1753 James Silvester the elder, to David Silvester - in consideration of his love and affection - 75 acres of land, part of "Grubby Neck" - lying in Tuckahoe Neck at the head of the Horsepen Branch. Wit: G. Pemberton, N. Wright. Acknowledged before Jonathon Nicols and Nathan Wright. Alienation fine, three shillings sterling, paid to Richard Tilghman.

196. ___ October 1753 - 18 October 1753 Joshua Jacobs, Sawyer, to William Pryor, William Ridgaway and William Bennett - consideration 1,108 pounds of tobacco - twenty head of my best hoggs; two of my best beds and furniture; one heifer; two iron potts; all of my pewter and a gun - a chattel mortgage due 10 November next. Wit: Peter Maxwell. Acknowledged before Nathan Wright.

197. 9 May 1753 - 1 November 1753 Thomas Butler, Planter, to William Clayton, Gentleman - consideration ₤180 current money of Maryland - the northernmost moiety or one-half of "Chesterfield" - lying on the north side of Coursica Creek - the whole, 400 acres; as also one-half of "Tryangle," on the north side of Coursica Creek - adjoining the land of William Hemsley and Christopher Denny - 50 acres. A mortgage due 9 May 1756. Thomas and Sarah his wife (she being first privately examined) acknowledged before N. Wright and Nathan Wright.

199. 31 October 1753 - 3 November 1753 ADVERTISEMENT: Dennis Carey brought before me a stray mare, small and bay coloured - the owner paying costs and proving his property may inquire of Dennis Carey, living in Queen Ann's County about two miles from Tuckahoe Bridge. Jonathon Nicols.

199. 3 April 1750 - 15 November 1750 Daniel Cheston, late of Kent County, Province of Maryland, now of the City of Bristoll, England, Merchant, to Thomas Ringgold of Chester Town in Kent County (Md.) - Power of Attorney to sell a parcel of land in Cecill County called "Frisby's Farm" and part of "Frisby's Prime Choice" (purchased by me in fee from Thomas Bordley), also my messuage or tenement in Annapolis, Ann Arundell County (Md.), now in the possession of His Excellency, Samuel Ogle, present Governour (of Md.). Also to transfer my right and interest to a grist and saw mill on Red Lyon Branch by virtue of a mortgage made by James Robass of Queen Ann's County, Millwright. Wit: Jo. Beddome, J. Wade.
Philadelphia, 25 May 1750 John Beddome of Philadelphia, Merchant, was present with Joseph Wade and witnessed the writing of this Letter of Attorney - certified by William Peters, Jr., Justice of the Peace.

200. 19 May 1753 - 15 November 1753 Daniel Cheston of the City of Bris-

200. toll (Eng.), Merchant; by virtue of the within Power of Attorney to Thomas Ringgold, to Joshua Wollaston of New Castle County on Delaware, Innholder, and Richard Nicholas of the same place, Millwright - consideration ₤200 current money of the Province - twenty acres of land granted to James Robass for building a water mill on Red Lyon Branch - part of "Condon" and part of "Crompton" - and with a mill upon the land and run erected, together with all the wheels, houses, tackle, apparell, furniture and utensils to the same belonging. Thomas Ringgold acknowledged before James Brown and John Seegar.

201. 9 August 1753 - 17 January 1754 John Bruer and Elizabeth his wife, of St. Mary's County, Planter - the said Elizabeth Bruer being co-heir with Martha Rogers of Cecil County unto Agnes McKettrick, late relict of Dr. Andrew McKettrick of Kent County, Maryland, deceased - to Abraham Milton of Kent County, Planter - consideration ₤35.8.0 current money - 75 acres of land, lately owned by Dr. Andrew McKittrick, one-half of 150 acres called "Crump's Forrest" - lying on the east side of the southwest branch of Island Creek. Wit: Gilbert Ireland, Justinian Jordan, before whom the deed was acknowledged - certified Justices of the Peace for St. Mary's County (Md.) by Richard Ward Key, Clerk. Alienation fine, three shillings sterling.

204. 14 September 1753 - 17 January 1754 William Rogers, Taylor, of Cecil County (Md.) and Martha his wife, to George Milligan of Cecil County - consideration ₤50 current money - all their right and interest in the land called "Marshall's Outlet" now called "Edinkelly," formerly in Kent County but now in Queen Ann's, by patent granted to Dr. Andrew McKettrick, 20 December 1749 for 600 acres. Acknowledged before P. Bayard and Adam Vanbebber, Justices of the Peace for Cecil County - certified by Matthew Bordley, Clerk. Alienation fine, twelve shillings sterling, paid to Richard Tilghman.

205. 7 November 1753 - 17 January 1754 John Brewer of St. Mary's County, Planter, and Elizabeth his wife (sister germain to the deceased Agnes McKettrick to whom the lands underwritten were solely devised by Dr. Andrew McKettrick, also deceased), to George Milligan of Cecill County, Merchant - consideration ₤20 sterling money of Great Britain and fifty shillings current - one-half of "Marshall's Out let," now "Edinkelly," formerly in Kent County but now in Queen Ann's, by patent granted to Dr. Andrew McKettrick, 20 December 1749 for 600 acres. Acknowledged before John Chesley and G. Ireland, Justices of the Peace for St. Mary's County - certified by Richard Ward Key, Clerk. Alienation fine, twelve shillings sterling paid to Richard Tilghman.

207. 17 January 1754 Charles Seth, Carpenter, to Dennis Carey, Planter - consideration ₤87 current money - 75 acres, part of "Bennett's Outlet," near the head of Back Wye River - adjoining "Forsett's Plains" and "Liberty," formerly possessed by William Mason. Acknowledged before John Downes, Jr. and John Downes . Rachel, wife of Charles Seth privately examined apart from her husband. Alienation fine, three shillings sterling.

209. 16 January 1754 - 24 January 1754 George Baynard, Planter, to Christopher Cross Ruth, Planter - consideration ₤34 paper currency of Maryland - 34 acres, part of "Baynard's Pasture," adjoining the dwelling plantation of Thomas Price and a tract called "Chestnut Meadow" - being part of a tract called "Hacker's Forrest," resurveyed some time ago by George Baynard and called "Baynard's Pasture." Acknowledged before Nathan Wright and N. Wright. Alienation fine, one shilling, four pence, half penny sterling, paid to Richard Tilghman.

210. 7 February 1754 Samuel Griffith, Saylor, to Emory Sudler, Planter - consideration ₤22 current money and 8,000 pounds of tobacco - 55 acres of land called "Little Neck" - lying on Kent Island on Broad Creek between the land of Phillip Connor, deceased, and a branch called Phillip's Branch. Acknowledged before Joseph Sudler and John Downes, Jr. Alienation fine, two shillings, two pence sterling.

211. 12 November 1753 - 7 February 1754 Dowdall Thompson, Planter, to Matthew Weeks, Planter - consideration ₤79 current money and 3,500 pounds of tobacco - 120 acres on the north side of Double Creek, called "Woolver Hamton." Dowdall and Hester his wife (she being first privately examined out of his hearing) acknowledged before James Brown and John Seegar. [Weeks also written "Wickes" within this same document.]

213. 12 November 1753 - 7 February 1754 Henry Lizinby, Planter, to Stephen Weeks, Planter - consideration 8,000 pounds of tobacco - 84 acres of land, part of a parcel sold by James Earle and William Turbutt for the payment of the debts of Robert Smith, Esquire, to John Weeks, father of Stephen - part of two tracts lying on the east side of Double Creek - one being "Mt. Pleasure" otherwise "Mt. Pleasant," the other, "Enjoyment" otherwise "Linngston's Enjoyment" - being the southernmost part of the parcel. Acknowledged before James Brown and John Seegar.

214. 4 December 1753 - 21 February 1754 William Whitby to Joseph Whitby - gift of love - 100 acres called "Buck Range," in the Forrest of Choptank - near a road leading from the head of Chester to the head of Choptank River on the east side thereof and opposite the Bee Tree Swamp. Acknowledged before William Hopper and Jonathon Nicols. Alienation fine, four shillings sterling, paid to Richard Tilghman.

215. 12 November 1753 - 14 March 1754 Stephen Weeks, Planter, to Henry Lizenby, Planter - consideration 8,000 pounds of tobacco - 80 acres of land, part of "Mt. Pleasant" otherwise "Mt. Pleasure" - adjoining "Tilghman's Discovery." Stephen and Ann his wife (she being first privately examined) acknowledged before James Brown and John Seegar. Alienation fine, three shillings, two pence, half penny sterling.

216. 12 November 1753 - 14 March 1754 Stephen Weeks, Planter, to Dowdall Thompson - consideration ₤52.10.0 current money - 52½ acres, part of

216. "Mt. Pleasant" otherwise "Mt. Pleasure." Acknowledged before James Brown and John Seegar. Alienation fine, two shillings, twp pence, half penny sterling, paid to Richard Tilghman.

218. 11 October 1753 - 14 March 1754 James Roseberry, Planter, and Mary his wife, to James Ware, Blacksmith - consideration ₤38 current money - 67 acres of land, part of "Brotherhood" - lying on the west side of "Clouds' Adventure." James and Mary (she being first privately examined out of hearing of her husband) acknowledged before James Brown and Nathan Wright. Alienation fine, two shillings, eight pence, half penny sterling.

219. 21 March 1754 Certificate of Estray: William Durding brought before me a small black mare about five years old, trespassing on him. The owner paying costs and proving his property can take her away. John Downes.

219. 13 March 1754 - 25 March 1754 Charles Gafford, Senior, Planter, to Charles Gafford, Junior, Carpenter - consideration 5,000 pounds of tobacco - part of "Macklain," on the main road leading from Collins' Mill to St. Andrew's Chappell, containing 118 acres; part of "Smithfield," 40 acres adjoining - lying on the west side of Red Lyon Branch. Acknowledged before James Brown and John Seegar. Alienation fine, six shillings, four pence sterling, paid to Richard Tilghman.

220. 22 September 1753 - 26 March 1754 James Harvey and James Carter, qualified by Joseph Sudler to estimate the value of "Connor's Neck," in the possession of James Walters, guardian to Susanna and Elizabeth Connor, orphans to Nathaniel Connor, deceased - entered upon the land and found two dwelling houses, old and out of repair; one tobacco house, out of repair; one corn house; one 30 feet tobacco house; nineteen apple trees; forty peach trees; nine cherry trees; 2,000 (?) of fencing; one parcel of old fencing. The guardian is not permitted to clear more than from the head of Cool Spring Branch to the Tarkill Cornfield and with the fence to the main road to where his gate now stands; he is permitted to get timber for necessary repairs, rails and tobacco hogsheads - the rent, 400 pounds of tobacco annually.

221. 20 December 1753 - 27 March 1754 We have viewed and valued two tracts of land belonging to James Stephens, son of John Stephens, his guardian, Nicholas Linch, being qualified by Joseph Sudler. On the land called "Stephens' Adventure" on Kent Island we found one dwelling house, 24 feet long, 20 feet wide, 10 feet pitch, with posts in the ground, one brick gable end and chimney, good plank floors and doors and a good cover of drawn boards and the said house in good repair; also a citchin (sic!), 16 feet square, chestnut loggs, hewed and duftailed (sic!), a brick chimney and tolerable good cover; also a milk house, 8 feet square and 6 feet pitch, framed and in bad repair; a tobacco house, 30 feet long, 20 feet wide, ruff (sic!) work, in bad repair; two small corn houses, not worth repairing; a small young orchard of 47 trees; the plantation in tolerable good repair of

221. fencing; the guardian is not permitted to clear any more land and to get timber only for necessary repairs; the rent, 600 pounds of tobacco per annum. On "Tarkill," one old logg'd dwelling house, not worth repairing; one old corn house; a small parcel of old fence. Rent, 100 pounds of tobacco per annum. S. Blunt, Jr., James Walters.

221. 17 March 1754 - 27 March 1754 Henry Feddeman and Francis Stevens, nominated by John Downes to value the land of William Sharp, late of Talbot County (Md.), deceased, in behalf of the orphan Henry Sharp, entered into the land and found one dwelling house, 20 feet long, 16 feet wide in good repair; one dwelling house not worth repairing; one tobacco house, 30 feet long, 22½ feet wide in pretty good repair; one corn house, 10 feet long, 7 feet wide and one corn house, 10 feet long, 7 feet wide, both in good repair; 32 very small apple trees; the fencing all in good repair. Peter Cummerford, the guardian, is to cut timber and clear fifty acres of land; the rent, 500 pounds of tobacco yearly; Cummerford is to build a dwelling house of hew'd loggs, covered with boards of 20 feet in length and 16 feet broad, finished workmanlike, the boards drawn and sapt, and pay the quitrents.

222. 9 June 1753 - 28 March 1754 Lawrence Hall and John Bracco, qualified before Jonathon Nicols to estimate the yearly value of the land of Benjamin Griffin, orphan son of Benjamin Griffin, deceased; John Sweat, Jr., his guardian - find about 16 acres cleared, fenced in with 544 pannells of fencing, one-half whereof is very old rails; one old 40 feet tobacco house, entirely useless and incapable of being repaired; the whole plantation containing 208½ acres of land, a part of "Lloyd's Park," per a certificate of division made by John Coursey between John Sweat, Jr. in behalf of the abovenamed orphan and Matthew Griffin, his uncle; John Sweat is to clear 44 acres more adjoining the cultivation. We find the orphan to be lame in such a manner as to render him incapable of any bodily labour; that he is likewise deaf and dumb; and his father, having by report of John Sweat, Jr., left no personal estate after payment of his debts. John Sweat, Jr. holds one-third interest in the right of his wife, mother of the said orphan and being of necessity obliged to build thereon in order to reap any advantage from the occupation thereof and the said orphan being now fifteen years of age, so that Sweat hath but a small time to make use of the said plantation, which must cost him a considerable expense and trouble to make - we value the land and improvements worth no more than the quitrents besides keeping and maintaining the orphan during his minority.

223. 13 March 1754 - 28 March 1754 Charles Gafford, Sr., Planter, to Richard Gafford, Carpenter - consideration 5,000 pounds of tobacco - a parcel of land called "Macklain," 141 acres on the road from Collins' Mill to St. Andrew's Chappell, and 17 acres adjoining, called "Smithfield," on the west side of Red Lyon Branch. Acknowledged before James Brown and John Seegar. Alienation fine, six shillings, four pence sterling, paid to Richard Tilghman.

224. 11 November 1753 - 29 March 1754 John Johnston, Bricklayer and Planter, to John Pipen, Planter, and Rebecca his wife - lease for seven years from date of "Bee Tree Rige (sic!)" - the rent being 500 pounds of tobacco per annum. Pipen to build a twenty-feet log house, eighteen feet wide with hued (sic!) logs, provided Johnston finds a hand to hue (sic!) them - Johnston to find nails to build the house. The said Pipen agrees not to allow any other person to use the land or to cut timber except for cessary repairs. Wit: N. Cleave, Samuel Bostick.

225. 30 March 1754 - 4 April 1754 Benjamin Denny, Planter, to George Cope, Planter - consideration ₤250 current - a parcel of land called "Denny's Range," as per the patent, issued 14 April 1748. Benjamin and Susannah his wife (she being first privately examined) acknowledged before Jo. Smyth and John Bracco. Alienation fine, four shillings sterling, paid to Richard Tilghman.

226. 26 March 1754 - 9 April 1754 John Hawkins and Sarah his wife, to Edward Browne - consideration 1,000 pounds of tobacco and 40 shillings current money - all their lots in Ogletown with all improvements. Acknowledged before John Downes, Jr. and John Seegar.

227. 26 February 1754 - 18 April 1754 Gideon Swift, Planter, to Thomas Marsh, Gentleman - consideration 4,000 pounds of tobacco and ₤20 - 150 acres of land called "Lowther's Chance" - lying in the borders of Queen Ann's County, formerly granted to Henry Lizenby. Gideon and Ann his wife (she being first privately examined) acknowledged before James Brown and John Seegar. Alienation fine, six shillings sterling.

228. 28 May 1754 - 30 May 1754 Certificate of Estray: Nicholas Griffin brought before me a middle sized bay horse with a star in his forehead, in middling order and the present owner unknown. Robert Lloyd.

228. 17 May 1754 - 30 May 1754 James Hobbs, Planter, to Charles Browne, Merchant - consideration ₤80 - 281 acres called "Hobbs' Venture," on the north side of Cow Marsh on a branch of Choptank River. Acknowledged before Jonathon Nicols and John Bracco. Alienation fine, eleven shillings, three pence sterling, paid to Richard Tilghman.

229. 26 May 1754 - 6 June 1754 John Loyd, Planter, to John Atkinson, Jr. - consideration 10,000 pounds of tobacco and ₤10 current money - 132 acres of land, part of "Tom's Fancy Enlarged" - lying in Tully's Neck. John and Rebecca his wife (she being first privately examined) acknowledged before William Hopper and Nathan Wright. Alienation fine, five shillings, four pence sterling.

230. ADVERTISEMENT: 12 June 1754 George Jeffrys brought before me a small mare, between a bay and roan with a black mane and tail - the owner may apply to Jeffrys, proving his property and paying costs. John Bracco.

231. 24 June 1754 Thomas Barns and William Joyner, qualified before John Smyth, Esquire to make a just estimate of the value of some land on Kent Island called "Allan's Deceit," belonging to William Kirby, a minor, his guardian, Henary Carroll - on 15 May instant, entered into the land and found one dwelling house, 40 by 20 feet, brick gable ends, shingled, very much out of repair, not plaistered; one tobacco house, 40 by 20 feet, very much out of repair; one kitching (sic!), 20 by 18 feet, much out of repair; one, 16 by 12 feet, new covered; one logg frame (house?), 20 by 8 feet, duftaild; 360 apple trees; 13 cherry trees; 69 peach trees; 2 aprecock (sic!) trees; one English walnut tree; 1927 pannells of fencing; the rent, ₤12 paper currency of the Province. The guardian to get boards and shingles for repairs and build a new tobacco house; also for fencing anywhere on the land and clear all woods inside the run that runs from Ellexander Walters' fence down to the brook and no further.

231. 29 April 1754 - 26 June 1754 Jacob Bayley, Planter, to James Ringgold of Eastern Neck in Kent County (Md.), Gentleman - consideration ₤50 current money - 50 acres, part of "Bishop's Outlet" - north side of Coursica Creek - adjoining James Ringgold's purchase of Nathan Samuel Turbutt Wright and Thomas Wright, and the lands belonging to Charles Raley. Sig: Jacob "Baley." Acknowledged before Richard Tilghman, Justice of the Provincial Court. Alienation fine, two shillings sterling, paid to Richard Tilghman.

234. 26 June 1754 Vinson Benton and Abner Dudley, appointed by Dowdall Thompson to value the land of John Johnson, Jr., son of Albert Johnson, now in possession of Benjamin Blower, his guardian - on 13 April instant, entered upon the land, two adjoining tracts, one called "Lawrence's Delight," the other, "Johnson's Addition," and found one dwelling house, 30 feet in length and 18 feet in width, shingled but to be covered with featheredged shingles; also a tobacco house, 40 feet in length and 21 feet in width; one out house of littel (sic!) value; the fencing in middling repair; 174 apple trees under good fencing - the guardian is not permitted to clear any land and may get timber for repairs and firewood. Rent, 300 pounds of tobacco per annum.

234. 27 June 1754 Nathaniel Wright, Gentleman, to Nathan Wright the younger, and Thomas Baley, the younger - consideration five shillings - one negro slave named "Jack" - they to pay William Anderson, Jonathon Nicols & Company the sum and costs of a judgment, on or before 10 February next. [Nathaniel Wright signed thus: "N. Wright."] Acknowledged before Nathan Wright and John Downes, Jr.

235. 8 June 1754 - 6 July 1754 Joseph Denny of Talbot County, Planter, and Rebecca his wife, to Richard Mansfield, Carpenter - an exchange of 128 acres in Tuckahoe Neck called "Turner's Plains" for 134 3/4 acres, parts of two tracts called "UppHolland" and "Wisbitch" - lying on the west side of Broad Creek in Talbot County - adjoining the land called "Mable." Wit: William Goldsborough, Thomas Brereton, James Earle. Joseph and Rebecca (she being first privately exam-

235. ined) acknowledged before William Goldsborough, Justice of the Provincial Court. Alienation fine, five shillings, one pence, half penny sterling, paid to Richard Tilghman.

236. 27 June 1754 - 1 August 1754 Thomas Cloak and Rebecker (sic!) his wife, to Josias Sollaway - consideration 2,000 pounds of tobacco and ₺5 paper currency - 50 acres of land, part of "Cloak's Chance" - lying between Andover and the Unicorn Branches - on the west side of the road leading from Maurise Cloak's plantation to Robart Phillips' Landing. Thomas and Rebecca (she being first privately examined) acknowledged before William Hopper and John Downes, Jr. Alienation fine, two shillings sterling.

237. 23 July 1754 - 15 August 1754 William Timm, Planter, to James Slaughter, Planter - consideration ₺20 - 50 acres called "Goldenrodridge," in the Forrest of Choptank - adjoining a tract formerly laid out for James Loydell called "Swine's Paradise." Acknowledged before Jonathon Nicols and John Bracco. Alienation fine, two shillings sterling. [The grantor's name also written thus within the document - "Tymm."]

239. 13 June 1754 - 15 August 1754 Anne Meredith, Widow, to Dennis Carey, Planter - 100 acres of land called "Middle Plantation" - reference made to a Writ of Entry obtained by Carey against Anne Meredith, third Tuesday of May last concerning one-half of the land. Wit: Richard Tilghman, Charles Seth. Acknowledged before Richard Tilghman, Justice of the Provincial Court.

240. 15 August 1754 John Camper, Planter, to Edward Tilghman, Gentleman - consideration 7,091 pounds of tobacco - one-third of "Reviving Spring" on Unicorn Branch - the whole being 500 acres. John and Sarah his wife (she being first privately examined) acknowledged before Robert Lloyd and William Tilghman. Alienation fine, five shillings, eight pence sterling.

240. 15 August 1754 Richard Tilghman, Esquire, to Edward Tilghman, Gentleman - consideration ₺38.10.0 current money - 50 acres of land called "Bever Dambs" (sic!) - lying on the west side of the Bever Damb Branch (sic!), a little above the road that leads through the forrest to the Horsehead. Also 50 acres called the "Hollow Flatt," lying on the east side of Beaver Dam Branch, below Tom Jones' Pond. Acknowledged before Robert Lloyd and William Tilghman. Alienation fine, four shillings sterling.

242. 22 August 1754 - 23 August 1754 John Johnson, Planter, to Francis Rochester, Planter - consideration ₺220 current money - 300 acres, part of "Ripply." Wit: John Nevill, George Garnett. John and Sarah his wife (she being first privately examined) acknowledged before Robert Lloyd. Alienation fine, twelve shillings sterling. [John signed the deed thus: John Johnson, Ripley.]

243. 22 August 1754 - 23 August 1754 John Johnson, Planter, to Thomas Teat, Planter - consideration ₺35 current money - 50 acres called

243. "Bee Tree Ridge" - lying in the Forrest of Choptank, near Chickens Marsh, issuing out of the main branch of Tuckahoe Creek called the Long Marsh. Wit: John Nevill, George Garnett. Acknowledged before Robert Lloyd.

244. 7 August 1754 - 27 August 1754 Richard Mansfield of Talbot County, Carpenter, and Elizabeth his wife, to William Oxenham - consideration ₺96 current money - 128 acres called "Turner's Plains" - adjoining "Edmondson's Green Close." Wit: William Goldsborough, Patrich Makway. Richard and Elizabeth (she being first privately examined out of his hearing) acknowledged before William Goldsborough, Justice of the Provincial Court. Alienation fine, five shillings, one pence, half penny sterling, paid to Richard Tilghman.

245. 7 May 1754 - 27 August 1754 John Nevill, Planter, to Benjamin Whittington, Farmer - consideration ₺270 current - 234 acres, part of "Poplar Hill," on the south side of Chester River. John and Katherine his wife (she being first privately examined), acknowledged before Nathan Wright and Dowdall Thompson. Alienation fine, four shillings, eight pence sterling.

247. 23 July 1754 - 28 August 1754 Absalom Jumpe and Solomon Jumpe, Planters, to Henry Casson, Merchant - consideration ₺36.17.0 current money - 129 acres of land, part of "Jumpe's Chance" - lying on the east side of the main branch of Tuckahoe Creek - bequeathed to Absalom by the will of his father, William Jumpe. Also 6 acres, part of the same land, bequeathed by William Jumpe to his son, Solomon Jumpe. Acknowledged before Jonathon Nicols and John Bracco. Alienation fine, five shillings, ten pence sterling.

248. 16 May 1754 - 29 August 1754 Benjamin Whittington, Farmer, to Thomas Marsh, Gentleman - consideration ₺57.13.10 current money - 50 acres of land, part of "Poplar Hill" - lying on the main road that leads from Kings Town to Collins' Mill. Wit: Dennis Dulany, Richard Lloyd. Benjamin and Jane his wife (she being first privately examined), acknowledged before Robert Lloyd, Justice of the Provincial Court. Alienation fine, one shilling sterling.

250. 7 September 1754 - 9 September 1754 John Offly Collins, Planter, to Andrew Hall, Merchant - consideration ₺35 current money - 35 acres, part of "Spread Eagle" - lying on the Southeast Branch of Chester River and on Collins' Mill Branch - adjoining a part sold to John Smyth and a part sold by Benjamin Hines to Andrew Hall. John and Sarah his wife (she being first privately examined), acknowledged before James Brown and Dowdall Thompson. Alienation fine, one shilling, ten pence sterling, paid to Richard Tilghman.

252. 7 September 1754 - 9 September 1754 John Offley Collins, Planter, to John Smyth, Chirurgeon Apothecary - consideration ₺71 current - and 6,000 pounds of tobacco - 71 acres of land, part of "Spread Eagle" - lying on the Southeast Branch - on the south side of a millpond called Collins' Millpond. John and Sarah (she being first

252. privately examined out of his hearing), acknowledged before James Brown and Dowdall Thompson. Alienation fine, two shillings, ten pence, half penny sterling, paid to Richard Tilghman.

253. 29 August 1754 Charles Mooney, Planter, to Edward Tilghman - in order to secure a bond in the amount of Ŀ40 paper money of Maryland (formerly held by John Johnson (of "Riply") who has since sold his plantation and has absconded) - in consideration of the sum of five shillings - these chattels now on my dwelling plantation: one white mare about ten years old; one iron gray mare; one black horse about nine years old; five cows; two heifers; two calves; seven sheep, all but one I bought of Thomas Monsieur; four sows, one with seven pigs; fourteen spayed sows and barrows; nine shoats; four featherbeds, one I lent to my sister, wife of Richard Moore and all it's covering; one small pine chest; one large pine chest; one poplar chest; three iron potts; six pewter dishes; twelve pewter plates; all of the wheat now in the straw and all of the corn and tobacco now growing. Wit: Christopher Wilkinson, Thomas Teat. Acknowledged before James Brown.

254. 6 September 1754 - 12 September 1754 Maurice Cloak of Kent Island, Province of Maryland, Planter, to Joseph Sudler, Merchant - consideration Ŀ15 current money - 50 acres called "Tilbury's Addition," on Davenishes Branch, near the head thereof, issuing out of the Unicorn Branch. Acknowledged before James Brown and Dowdall Thompson. Alienation fine, two shillings sterling, paid to Richard Tilghman.

255. 6 September 1754 - 12 September 1754 Thomas Cloak, Planter, to Joseph Sudler, Merchant - consideration Ŀ15 current money - 100 acres, part of "Cloak's Chance" - on the west side of the road that leads from Maurice Cloak's plantation to Robert Phillips' Landing (of which 50 acres was sold to Josias Sollaway). Thomas and Rebecca his wife (she being first privately examined), acknowledged before James Brown and Dowdall Thompson. Alienation fine, two shillings sterling.

256. 14 September 1754 - 16 September 1754 James Hammond, Planter, to James Williams Nabb, Planter - in consideration of 192 acres of land, part of "Wrench'es Adventure," made over by James Williams Nabb and Elizabeth his wife - grants 172 acres of land called "Moor's Hope Addition" - adjoining "Miss Hit," formerly surveyed for Stephen Rich, lying on Coursica Creek branch called Chester Mill Branch. James and Rachel his wife (she being first privately examined out of his hearing), acknowledged before William Hopper and Nathan Wright. Alienation fine, six shillings, eleven pence sterling.

257. 9 September 1754 - 18 September 1754 William Joyner of Kent Island, to Edward Lloyd of Talbot County - consideration Ŀ100 paper currency - a tract of land called "Cooper's Hill" - lying on Kent Island (by patent said to lye in Kent County) on the south side of Long Creek - 100 acres laid out for William Joyner, deceased, father of the above William Joyner by assignment from Henry Parker who had the said 100 acres assigned to him by Bryan Omaley, out of a warrant

257. granted to him for 1,050 acres - patented 19 May 1710. Acknowledged before John Smyth and John Bracco. Alienation fine, four shillings sterling.

259. 15 April 1754 - 19 September 1754 Alexander Meconekin, Labourer, to Daniel Meconekin, Planter - consideration 500 pounds of tobacco - 150 acres of land called "Meconekin's Correar," adjoining "Boothsby Fortune" - between the Unicorn Branch and the head of Chester River Branch. Acknowledged before Nathan Wright, and Dowdall Thompson.

260. 14 September 1754 - 19 September 1754 James Williams Nabb, Planter, and Elizabeth his wife, to James Hammond, Planter - consideration ɫ30 current money and 10,800 pounds of tobacco and a negro woman slave named "Sarah;" one black riding mare and 172 acres of land, part of Moor's Hope Addition" - conveys 192 acres of land, part of "Wrench'es Adventure" - lying on the road that leads from the free school down the neck to Nathan Samuel Turbutt Wright's - all of the remaining part unsold to Charles Downes. James and Elizabeth (she being first privately examined), acknowledged before William Hopper and Nathan Wright. Alienation fine, seven shillings, eight pence, half penny sterling, paid to Richard Tilghman.

261. 18 September 1754 - 26 September 1754 Thomas Wilkinson, Planter, to Christopher Wilkinson - consideration ɫ6 sterling, ɫ30 currency and 2,000 pounds of tobacco - one brown mare about eleven years old; one small bay mare, about eleven; two cows about six years; one bull, four years old; one heifer and two yearlings; one large walnut table; four small walnut tables; one bed and furniture; five pewter dishes; one hand mill; two iron potts; two wooling and linnen wheels; two small looking glasses; one midling looking glass. Acknowledged before Nathan Wright.

262. 24 September 1754 - 3 October 1754 Daniel Hamer of Kent County, Province of Maryland, Taylor and James Tilghman, Gentleman, of Talbot County, to James Massey, Cordwinder - 118½ acres of land; one-half of "Smith's Delight," 200 acres; and "Hammour's Addition," 34 acres - allotted to Ezekial Hamer by a deed of partition between Ezekial and Richard Ponder and Sarah his wife, dated 11 September 1727. Mention a Writ of Entry obtained from the Provincial Court. Wit: Charles Scott, William Hynson of Kent County. Acknowledged by Daniel and Anne his wife (she being first privately examined), before Scott and Hynson; certified by James Smith, Clerk of Kent County.
27 September 1754 James Tilghman acknowledged before William Goldsborough, Justice of the Provincial Court.

263. 8 October 1754 - 9 October 1754 William Manning to William Cannon, Planter - consideration 5,000 pounds of tobacco - one mare, called a chestnut rone (sic!); one dark iron gray mare, seven years old; seven old hoggs; twelve piggs; eighteen shoats; two cows had from John Davis, Sr.; two calves belonging to the two cows; one brown cow bought of John Williams; the crop of corn growing on the plantation; all of the fodder and all of the tobacco that is housed or may be

263. housed hereafter on that plantation where I now dwell; all of my wheat; all of the old corn; one plow and irons; a pair of leading lines; one colter; two iron potts and pothooks; one bed of country linnen tick and a featherbed furniture; two chests; four axes; one grubbing hoe; one drawing knife; three iron wedged; three weeding hoes; two hilling hoes and all utensils belonging to my house. Wit: Thomas Marsh, Thomas Price.

263. 25 March 1754 - 18 October 1754 James Silvester, Planter, to his son, William Silvester - consideration love and affection - 75 acres, part of "Grubby Neck" - lying in Tuckahoe Neck on the head of Horsepen Branch. Acknowledged before Jonathon Nicols and John Bracco. Alienation fine, three shillings sterling, paid to Richard Tilghman.

264. 21 October 1754 John Young (son of John Young) to Nathaniel Scott, Jr. - consideration 5,500 pounds of tobacco - part of "Stratton," conveyed from Richard Bennett, Esquire, to John Young, 18 July 1746 for 54½ acres. John and Mary his wife (she being first privately examined), acknowledged before Nathan Wright and John Bracco.

265. 2 November 1754 - 7 November 1754 John Wootters, Planter, to John Barwick of Talbot County, Planter - consideration ₺30 current money of Maryland - 47½ acres, part of "Jumpe's Choice" - lying in the fork between Tuckahoe Creek and Choptank River - on the south side of St. Jones's Path. Acknowledged before Jonathon Nicols and John Bracco. Alienation fine, one shilling, eleven pence sterling.

266. 2 November 1754 - 7 November 1754 Phillip Palmer of Talbot County, Joyner, and Rose his wife, to John Barwick, Planter, of Talbot County - consideration 1,600 pounds of tobacco - 17 acres, part of "Jumpe's Choice" - one-third of 50 acres sold by William Jumpe to William Barwick of Talbot County. Phillip and Rose (she being first privately examined) acknowledged before Jonathon Nicols and John Bracco.

268. 8 May 1754 - 7 September 1754 Peter Rich of Dorchester County, to William Hughlet and James Genn of Queen Ann's County - consideration ₺10 paper currency of the Province of Maryland - his right to a resurvey of "Rich's Farm" - 74 acres of land on the north side of the head of Great Choptank River - part of a special warrant granted to Peter Rich, 21 January 1750 and laid out 3 July 1751 - adjoining "Bakers Plains." Acknowledged before Jonathon Nicols and John Bracco. Alienation fine, three shillings sterling.

269. 4 November 1754 - 7 November 1754 George Herrington, Planter, to Philemon Green, Planter - consideration ₺25 current money - 55 acres, part of "Jones's Forrest" - lying on the north side of Muddy Branch, Choptank River - just below the plantation where John Teat formerly lived. Wit: Richard Tilghman, Alexander Williamson, Jr. Acknowledged before Richard Tilghman, Justice of the Provincial Court. Alienation fine, two shillings, two pence sterling.

270. 1 June 1754 - 21 November 1754 James Viney, Planter, to Nathaniel Wright the third - consideration 1,130 pounds of tobacco - one brindle cow; one cow calf; one black cow; one black and brown yearling; one 2-year old steer. Wit: James Roe, Francis Fallin.

271. 7 November 1754 - 21 November 1754 Henry Warren to James Anderson of Chester Town, Chyrurgeon - consideration ₤15.12.6 current money of Maryland - all my share of the tobacco, wheat and Indian corn on the plantation of the said James in Queen Ann's County, i.e. one-fifth of the tobacco and one-sixth of the corn and wheat - belonging to me as overseer on the said plantation over the labouring servants and slaves of the said James. Wit: Thomas Ringgold. Acknowledged before James Brown.

271. 2 September 1754 - 22 November 1754 Edward Jones, Planter, and Elizabeth his wife, to James Roberts, Planter - consideration 7,000 pounds of tobacco - 100 acres of land on the south side of Chester River - part of "Sandyhurst." Acknowledged by Edward and Elizabeth (she being first privately examined out of his hearing), before James Brown and Dowdall Thompson. Alienation fine, four shillings sterling, paid to Richard Tilghman.

273. 26 November 1754 William Horn and William Joyner, qualified by Dr. John Smyth to view and value the plantation on Kent Island called "Parson's Neck," belonging to Susanna Griffith, an orphan, her guardian, Edward Brown, Sr. - on 12 July entered upon the land and found a very good brick house, one story, 42 feet long, 22 feet wide, the under part plastered and panted; the outward roome panted blue; the chimney pease boxt and panted; two very good six-paneled doors; two shashes and three pear window shutters; one shash above one of the said doors, the said shashes containing 56 peans of glass, one of the same, broak. A very good closet with shelves round; a very good four-paneled door, panted. The inward roome, panted read and the chimney pease boxt; two shashes and three pears of window shutters containing 48 peans of glass, one broak. A very good closet, shelfed around and windows with six peans of lead glass and good two-panelled door; one door very indefrant; a very good planke partician, paneld and panted; a very good two-panneld door; a stoupe at the south door of the said house, six feet long, five feet wide and seats to the same. The upper parte of the said house, three rooms floor'd and two plank particians; three two-paneled doors; five dormant windows, three shashes containing 36 peans of glass, one of the same, broak; a very good stear and stear keas; the above dwelling house kivered with joynted shingels, wants new kivering; a brick seller under the said house, 22 feet wide and 18 feet long with a very good four-paneled door, panted, and a sorry outside door. A kitchen, 20 feet wide and 16 feet long, plank doors, brick chimney, boarded and kovered with feather edged shingels, wants repairing. A negro quarter, 24 feet by 18 feet, brick chimney, plank door and kivered with feather edged shingels, wants some boards outside; two very good logg houses, 12 feet square, kivered with feather edged plank and doors of the same. A small fram'd house, 8 feet square, kivered with

273. boards and a plank door, wants repairing. A small logg'd house, past repairing. A 40 feet by 18 feet tobacco house, kivered with feather edged shingels, wants repairing; a very good 40 feet by 20 feet tobacco house freame. A 30 feet by 20 feet tobacco house, kivered with boards, wants kivering. A small logg house, past repairing. A gowse house, 17 feet by 4 feet, 2 feet pitch, kivered with boards. A very good brick oven; a very good garden, 80 feet square and 240 feet of the same, paled and 80 feet, posts and reals. 800 pannels of indifrant fencing; 2,160 pannels of very indifrant fencing. 152 apple trees, 14 very old apple trees; 120 petch trees; 13 cherry trees; fower damson trees; fower peare trees; fower very small Inglish walnut trees; a nursery - - vizt: 4 small cherrie trees; 8 damson trees; 73 petch trees, very small. The guardian permitted to clear more land within the fence, nor no more on the plantation. Necessary firewood and timber for repairing. The annual value, ₤20 current money of Maryland yearly.

[Note: this entry was copied as it was written, and since it contains so many mis-spelled words, it would be futile to try and point them out - the reader may make his own interpretation! RBL.]

274. 27 November 1754 - 28 November 1754 Thomas Wilkinson, Gentleman, to Peter Maxwell, Planter - consideration 3,850 pounds of tobacco - 175 acres of land - a parcel called "Hazard" - adjoining "Sawyer's Forrest" - another piece called "Burton upon Wallises" - near the head of Wallises Creek - adjoining a parcel laid out for Henry Coursey - the land of Samuel Wright and the land called "Coursey's Range." Acknowledged before James Brown and John Bracco. Alienation fine, seven shillings sterling, paid to Richard Tilghman.

275. 15 November 1754 - 30 November 1754 Nathaniel Wright and Henry Wrench, qualified by John Bracco to value the land called "Wright's Chance," the right of John Wright, a minor, his guardian Henry Costin, Mariner - on 10 September entered upon the plantation and found one old logg house, 16 feet long, 16 feet wide, much out of repair; some few cherry trees, peach and apple trees, standing in an irregular form; about 35 acres cleared with very indifrent fencing to the same. The guardian to clear 35 acres to the northeast of the cleared ground lying by the plantation whereon Christopher Cross Routh now dwelleth, with liberty to cut timber for repairs. The annual value, 500 pounds of tobacco per annum exclusive of quitrents and repairs.

275. 20 July 1754 - 20 December 1754 James Butler and Sarah his wife, to Andrew Hall, Merchant - consideration ₤175 current money - 234 acres, part of "Brotherhood" - lying on the south side of Hambleton's Branch, Chester River - adjoining "Fox Harbour," "Fox Hill" and "Clouds' Adventure." James and Sarah his wife (she being first privately examined), acknowledged before James Brown and Dowdall Thompson. Alienation fine, nine shillings, four pence, half penny sterling.

277. 26 November 1754 - 4 December 1754 John Davis and Arthur Emory,

277. qualified by John Bracco to value the land called "Smith's Neglect," the right of John Ruth, his guardian, Thomas Butler - on 25 September entered upon the land and found a large old plantation all under fence and a fence across the plantation - the greatest part of the fencing old and mixed with many rotten rails; one old clapboard dwelling house, 24 feet long, 14 feet wide, very leaky; one out house, 16 feet long, 10 feet wide, old and leaky with many boards off; an old orchard with near fifty apple trees, several broken and decayed; the guardian is not permitted to clear exceeding 20,000 tobacco hills at common and reasonable distance in the whole nor to cut any timber but what shall be for necessary improvements and repairs and fencing; with liberty of firewood, hogshead timber for tobacco made on the plantation. The annual value, ₤3, exclusive of repairs and the quitrents.

277. 6 September 1754 - 4 December 1754 Benjamin Coventon and Thomas Jackson, appointed by Dowdall Thompson to value the plantation of Bexley Newnam, an orphan, William Newnam his guardian - entered upon the land and found one brick dwelling house, 30 feet long, 15 feet wide with a shed on one side in middling repair; one old logg smokehouse, 10 feet square; one old kitching, 20 feet long, 15 feet wide, with brick chimney; one old corn house, 15 feet long, 7 feet wide; one old tobacco house 40 feet in length, 20 feet in width; one new logged house, 12 feet long, 8 feet wide with a sellar under it; one old milk house, 15 feet long, 10 feet wide; one brick oven; one orchard of 120 bearing trees; 11 cherry trees; 7 quince trees; 900 pannels of fencing very indifferent. William Newnam to clear one acre and no more and get what rale (sic!) timber needed for the plantation and pay the quitrents.

278. 5 September 1754 - 5 December 1754 Henry Lizenby, Planter, to Dowdall Thompson, Planter - consideration ₤70 current money of the Province and 4,320 pounds of tobacco - 115 acres of land called "Parson's Chance" - lying on the south side of Chester River - adjoining land called "Tilghman's Discovery" on Beckells' Creek - also 80 acres adjoining, part of "Mt. Pleasant als Mt. Pleasure." Henry and Ann his wife (she being first privately examined out of his hearing) acknowledged before James Brown and John Smyth. Alienation fine, six shillings, two pence sterling, paid to Richard Tilghman.

279. 25 June 1754 - 17 December 1754 William Lucas of Talbot County, Planter, to John Whitby, Planter - consideration 4,000 pounds of tobacco - all his claim (by virtue of a devise in the will of Caleb Clark late of Talbot County) to a parcel of land called "Clarke's Lott" - lying on the east side of the main branch of Tuckahoe Creek and adjoining "Dickinson's Plains," 112 acres according to the survey made by Caleb Clarke, 9 May 1724. William and Sophia his wife (she being first privately examined) acknowledged before William Hopper and John Bracco. Alienation fine, four shillings, six pence sterling.

280. 23 September 1754 - 2 January 1755 William Covington to Nathaniel

280. Covington - consideration 6,000 pounds of tobacco and an exchange of 91 acres in Tully's Neck, part of "Hinsely's Plains" - assigns and sets over 140 acres adjoining, called "Covington's Necessity" and 37 acres, part of "Rachel's Desire." William and Sarah his wife (she being first privately examined out of his hearing) acknowledged before James Brown and Dowdall Thompson. Alienation fine, seven shillings, one pence sterling, paid to Richard Tilghman.

282. 29 January 1755 - 4 February 1755 William Hill, Planter, to Thomas Story - consideration ₤10 current money - all of his household goods; a cow with Benjamin Insworth's mark; one yearling; two sows and nine piggs; one-third of the tobacco crop and three barrels of corn. Wit: John Bracco, Phebe Graham. Acknowledged before John Bracco.

282. 24 January 1755 - 4 February 1755 Notlar Harris, Widow, daughter and devisee of Nicholas Clouds, Planter, deceased, to James Tilghman of Talbot County, Attorney at Law - consideration ₤15 current money - 200 acres called "Kilkenny," on Andover Branch, Chester River. Wit: William Goldsborough, James Earle. Acknowledged before William Goldsborough, Justice of the Provincial Court. Alienation fine, eight shillings sterling, paid to Richard Tilghman.

283. 28 January 1755 - 4 February 1755 William Tarbutton, Planter, to George Baynard, Gentleman - consideration 4,500 pounds of tobacco - 100 acres, part of "Codshead Mannor," lying (as is supposed) partly in the head of Dorchester County and partly in the head of Queen Ann's County - on Fisher's Branch in Dorchester County. William and Rebecca his wife (she being first privately examined) acknowledged before Nathan Wright and John Bracco. Alienation fine, four shillings sterling.

284. 31 January 1755 - 4 February 1755 John Alley, Planter, to Richard Tilghman, Esquire - 110 acres, parts of two tracts of land, one called "Confusion," the other, "Adventure." Mention a Writ of Entry made against the land and a recovery thereof. John and Margaret his wife (she being first privately examined) acknowledged before William Tilghman and Nathan Wright.

285. 27 November 1754 - 6 February 1755 Charles Connor and Mary his wife, to Nicholas Clouds - consideration ₤28 current money of the Province and 2,500 pounds of tobacco - 16 acres of land on Kent Island, part of "Woodyard Thicket." Charles and Mary (she being first privately examined) acknowledged before Robert Lloyd and John Bracco.

287. 27 November 1754 - 6 February 1755 Charles Connor and Mary his wife, to Nicholas Clouds - consideration ₤14 current money and 1,250 pounds of tobacco - lease of 15 acres, part of "Woodyard Thicket" for a term of eight years and forty-five days from this date; with privilege of getting firewood from adjoining land. Charles and Mary acknowledged before Robert Lloyd and John Bracco.

288. 4 February 1755 - 13 February 1755 Dowdall Thompson, Gentleman, to

288. Peter Johnson, Planter - consideration 1,000 pounds of tobacco - 100 acres of land called "Lawrance's Delight" - lying near the little Red Lyon Branch - sold by Augustine Thompson to Henry Johnson, the deed bearing date of 23 January 1733 for 8,000 pounds of tobacco. The deed was not recorded as required by law and the land did revert and became the right of Dowdall Thompson. Acknowledged before James Brown and Nathan WRight. Alienation fine, four shillings sterling, paid to Richard Tilghman.

289. 19 August 1754 - 18 February 1755 Henry Covington, Planter, and Rachel his wife, to William Covington, Planter - consideration ₤37 current money - 37 acres, part of "Rachel's Desire." Henry and Rachel (she being first privately examined) acknowledged before Robert Lloyd and William Hopper. Signature on the deed, "Coventon."

290. 23 September 1754 - 17 February 1755 Nathaniel Covington to William Covington - in consideration for an exchange of 140 acres of land near "Hyndsley's Plains" called "Covington's Necessity" and 37 acres of land, part of "Rachel's Desire" - hath granted 91 acres, part of "Hyndsley's Plains" - lying in Tully's Neck, adjoining "Allcock's Pharsalia." Nathaniel and Mary his wife (she being first privately examined out of hearing of her husband) acknowledged before James Brown and Dowdall Thompson. Signature written "Coventon."

291. 4 February 1755 - 26 March 1755 John Seegar, Planter, to James Meanor, Carpenter - consideration 2,600 pounds of tobacco - 60 acres, part of "Seegar's Hazard." John and Elizabeth his wife (she being first privately examined) acknowledged before James Brown and Dowdall Thompson. Alienation fine, two shillings, five pence sterling, paid to Richard Tilghman.

292. 4 February 1755 - 26 March 1755 Morgan Ponder, Planter, to Benjamin Roberts, Planter - consideration 3,000 pounds of tobacco and ₤1 sterling money of Great Britain - 50 acres of land in the Long Neck near the Long Marsh, called "Watson's Desire." Acknowledged before James Brown and Dowdall Thompson. Alienation fine, two shillings sterling.

294. 26 March 1755 David Register, Blacksmith, and Margaret his wife, to Henry Hollyday of Talbot County, Gentleman - consideration ₤54 current money of the Province, ₤5 sterling money of Great Britain and 2,000 pounds of tobacco - 120 acres, part of "Turner's Plains Addition" - in Tuckahoe Neck (which was conveyed by a deed of exchange dated 26 January 1741 by Samuel Bartlett and Rachel his wife to Thomas Bartlett and on 22 April 1752 conveyed by Thomas Bartlett and Mary his wife to David Register). Wit: Thomas Emory, Richard Tilghman Earle. David and Margaret his wife (she being first privately examined) acknowledged before Richard Tilghman, Justice of the Provincial Court. Alienation fine, four shillings, ten pence sterling.

295. 26 March 1755 Lawrance Eavritt, Sr., Planter, to Lawrance Eavritt, Jr. - consideration ₤1.8.0 sterling money - 100 acres of land called "Eavritt's Content" - lying near Lowe's Marsh and a tract of land

295. called "Chance Hitt." Wit: Thomas Baggs, Richard Mason. Acknowledged by "Edward" Eavritt, Sr. before Robert Lloyd and Associate Justices. Receipt of four shillings sterling alienation fine was given to "Edward" Eavritt. Also written "Everitt."

296. 25 March 1755 - 27 March 1755 Thomas Richardson Roe, Planter, to Nathan Wright, Jr. - consideration £45 current money - mortgaged a negro man slave named "Will" until 10 May next. Wit: William Coursey, Sr., Nathan Wright.

297. 20 December 1754 - 29 March 1755 Marmaduke Goodhand and Charles Connor, qualified by Dr. John Smyth to value the land of James Sudler, an orphan under the care of Emory Sudler, his guardian - found one framed dwelling house, 20 feet square, shingled with featheredged shingles and weatherboarded with smooth boards, in good repair; a tobacco house 30 feet by 20 feet, posts in the ground, shingled and weatherboarded with ruff (sic!) boards below joyce (sic!), in good repair; one round logg henn house, 8 feet by 6 feet, covered with ruff boards; 490 pannels of fencing, indifferent good, 71 pannels very bad. The guardian to clear what land is inside the line on the southwest side of the plantation and likewise from the north corner on the east side of the cornfield to the tobacco house and to get rale (sic!) timber, hogshead timber or boards for the use of the plantation. The value is £3 currency per year and and the quitrents.

297. 11 March 1755 - 3 April 1755 Thomas Bayley, Planter, to Anne, wife of Benjamin Vanderford, his daughter - in consideration of his love and affection - 75 acres of land, part of "Bayley's Delight" - lying on the west side of a branch between where I now live and Benjamin Vanderford's. Wit: Thomas Wilkinson, John Hargidon. Thomas "Baley" acknowledged before Robert Lloyd and John Smyth. Alienation fine, three shillings sterling, paid to Richard Tilghman.

298. 11 March 1755 - 3 April 1755 Thomas Bayley to his daughter, Sarah Cheshire, wife of John Cheshire - a gift of love - the remainder of the land called "Bayley's Delight," after the gift to his daughter, Anne Vanderford - formerly called the "Adventure" and now resurveyed and patented. Acknowledged by Thomas "Baley" before Robert Lloyd and John Smyth. Alienation fine, three shillings sterling.

299. 27 February 1755 - 18 April 1755 Peter Johnson, Planter, to Thomas Harris, Gentleman - consideration 10,000 pounds of tobacco - 100 acres of land called "Johnson's Addition" and 100 acres called "Lawrance's Delight." Wit: N. Wright, Peter Maxwell. Peter acknowledged before John Downes, Jr. and John Smythe. On 27 March 1755 appeared Mary, wife of Peter Johnson, and acknowledged before John Downes, Jr. and Dowdall Thompson. Alienation fine, eight shillings sterling.

300. 19 April 1755 - 24 April 1755 This day John Seegar brought before me as a stray, a small dark brown mair (sic!) - branded. Dowdall

300. Thompson, Justice of the Peace.

300. 2 May 1755 This day Stephen Weeks brought before me a stray mear (sic!) of gray colour - branded. Dowdall Thompson.

300. 16 April 1755 - 1 May 1755 Francis Foreman and Sarah his wife, to his son, John Foreman - in consideration of the love and affection borne to him - the plantation on Royston Creek where he now lives and 100 acres of land adjacent to the said plantation. Wit: William Cropper, Daniel Smith, plant. (sic!).

300. 21 May 1755 - 22 May 1755 Absolam Tims, Planter, and Jane his wife, to Robert Brodey, Taylor - consideration ₤25 - 50 acres of land in the Forrest of Choptank, called "Sociaty Hill." Acknowledged before Robert Lloyd and John Downes, Jr. Alienation fine, two shillings sterling, paid to Richard Tilghman. [Brodey also written "Brodie"]

302. 21 May 1755 - 29 May 1755 Benjamin Blower, Blacksmith, to Foster Cunliffe, Ellis Cunliffe and Robert Cunliffe of Liverpool, Kingdom of Great Britain, Merchants - one servant man named Oliver Laseby, by trade a gunsmith with six years and upwards to serve, now in my possession - mortgaged for ₤26.9.2 current money of Maryland, payable with interest by 21 June next. Wit: James Brown, Jonathon Hall. Acknowledged before James Brown.

302. 29 May 1755 - 30 May 1755 William Permar of Newport, Colony of Rhode Island, to Anne Jacobs - consideration ₤50 current money of Maryland; in wheat at four shillings per bushel and Indian corn at two shillings per bushel - one negro woman slave named "Lettice," about twenty-two years of age. Wit: James Earle, William King.

303. 20 March 1755 - 12 June 1755 Hynson Wright, County of Beaufort, Province of North Carolina, Planter, and Sarah his wife, to Christopher Cox, Gentleman -consideration ₤250 current money of Pensilvania - 300 acres of land called "Low's Arcadia" - on a branch of Island Creek. Wit: George Johnston, H. B. Whitford, William Carruthers, Jr.
North Carolina: On 20 March 1755 before James Hassell, Chief Justice of the Province, at Newbern, Hynson Wright and Sarah his wife, (she being first privately examined) acknowledged their deed. Justice Hassell certified by Arthur Dobbs, Governor of the Province.

304. 16 June 1755 Vincent Tim and Catherine his wife, to George Tate - consideration 3,000 pounds of tobacco - 50 acres of land called "Tim's Arcadia" - lying in Choptank Forrest at the Two Mile Pond, issuing out of Old Town Branch. Wit: Richard Tilghman, John Sayer Blake. Vincent and Catherine (she being first privately examined) acknowledged before Richard Tilghman, Justice of the Provincial Court. Alienation fine, two shillings sterling.

305. 20 May 1755 - 24 June 1755 John Scrivener, Cooper, to Henry Runnels, Planter - lease of land to clear for a plantation for a term

305. of seven years - Runnels not to cut the timber except for use of the plantation; John Scrivener obliges to build a tobacco house and a dwelling house for Runnels and Henry Runnels to pay rent of 600 pounds of tobacco after two years rent free - if not, paying a forfit (sic!) of 4,000 pounds of tobacco. Wit: Robert Thomas, John Beale, Joseph Scrivener.

306. 20 June 1755 - 24 June 1755 Archabald Jackson to his son, Archabald Jackson, Jr. - in consideration of the love and affection borne to him - 113 acres of land called "Nodd" - lying on the west side of the main branch of Choptank River. Acknowledged before John Bracco and Jonathon Nicols. Alienation fine, four shillings, six pence, half penny sterling, paid to Richard Tilghman.

306. 20 June 1755 - 24 June 1755 Archabald Jackson to his son, James Jackson - in consideration of the love and affection borne to him - 100 acres of land, part of a tract called "Ratcliffe." Acknowledged before Jonathon Nicols and John Bracco. Alienation fine, four shillings sterling.

307. 20 June 1755 - 24 June 1755 Archabald Jackson to his son, Abednego Jackson - in consideration of the love and affection borne to him - 100 acres of land, part of a tract called "Ratcliffe" - adjoining "Old Town." Acknowledged before Jonathon Nicols and John Bracco. Alienation fine, four shillings sterling.

308. 24 June 1755 William Thomas of Talbot County to George Personett - consideration ₶40 current money of the Province - 80 acres of land, part of "Smith's Range" - lying on the branches of Island Creek - granted to Robert Smith, 3 July 1682, at the time in Talbot County - conveyed to Walter Riddle by Smith, 17 June 1691; and Riddle dying without issue, the land fell to his sister Jane and after her death to her son, William Thomas. Acknowledged before Nathan Wright and Dowdall Thompson. Alienation fine, three shillings, two pence, half penny sterling, paid to Richard Tilghman.

309. 15 April 1755 - 25 June 1755 John Sullivane, Planter, and Sarah his wife, to Thomas Clayland - consideration ₶116.5.0 current money of Maryland - 116 1/4 acres, part of "Dungarnon" (formerly lying in Talbot County). John and Sarah (she being first privately examined) acknowledged before James Brown and Dowdall Thompson. Alienation fine, four shillings, nine pence sterling.

310. 20 June 1755 - 25 June 1755 William Mountague, Planter, and Anne his wife, to Thomas Baggs, Planter - consideration ₶12 current - part of "Ratcliffe," lying in the Forrest of Choptank - adjoining "Chance Hitt." (No acreage given). William and Anne (she being first privately examined) acknowledged before Jonathon Nicols and John Bracco. Alienation fine, one shilling, nine pence sterling.

311. 25 June 1755 - 26 June 1755 Edward Clayton to John Tillotson - 160 acres of land called "Sheppard's Folds." Mention a Writ of Entry and

311. recovery of the same. Acknowledged before James Brown and John Downes, Jr. Alienation fine, six shillings, five pence sterling, paid to Richard Tilghman.

312. 23 June 1755 - 26 June 1755 Absolam Timm and Jane his wife, to Robert Brodey, Taylor - consideration ₤12.10.0 current money of the Province - 25 acres, part of "Sociaty Hill's Addition" - adjoining "Sociaty Hill," now in the possession of Robert Brodey. Wit: Richard Tilghman, Alexander Williamson, Jr. Absolam and Jane (she being first privately examined out of his hearing) acknowledged before Richard Tilghman, Justice of the Provincial Court. Alienation fine, one shilling sterling.

314. 25 June 1755 - 27 June 1755 Thomas Wilkinson, and William Carmichall to John Wilkinson - consideration ₤700 current money - 350 acres of land called "Barbadoes Hall." Reference to a Writ of Entry involving Carmichall. Acknowledged before James Brown and Dowdall Thompson.

315. 15 February 1755 - 10 July 1755 Lewis Deroachburne of Kent Island, Planter, to John Matthews, Taylor, and Catherine his wife - a lifetime lease of their dwelling plantation and one acre of land - Lewis to provide them with pasture for two head of cattle; liberty of cutting firewood and rail timber for fencing a garden. Wit: Nicholas Swormstedt, Jr., Samuel Blunt, James Hutchings. Acknowledged before Richard Tilghman, Justice of the Provincial Court.

316. 14 July 1755 - 17 July 1755 This day Edward Young brought before me a stray black mare, about four years old. Dowdall Thompson.

316. 17 July 1755 - 21 July 1755 This day William Cropper on Chester River brought before me a stray rone (sic!) horse. Dowdall Thompson.

316. ADVERTISEMENT. 21 July 1755 - 24 July 1755 At the plantation of James Lane, Jr. near his Lordship's Mannor, a middle sized sorrel mare, taken up as a stray. The owner may apply to James Lane, proving his property and paying costs. John Bracco.

316. ADVERTISEMENT. 22 July 1755 - 24 July 1755 William Winchester Mason has brought before me a stray, small gray horse, about seven or eight years old - has brand marks. The owner applying to Mason, proving his property and paying charges, may take him. John Bracco.

316. 25 July 1755 William Campbell, Planter, to Christopher Cox, Planter - consideration ₤24 current money and ₤12 Pensilvania currency - 40 acres formerly lying in Talbot County, called "Walker's Square." Wit: Richard Tilghman, Alexander Williamson, Jr. Acknowledged before Richard Tilghman. Alienation fine one shilling, seven pence, half penny sterling.

317. 9 June 1755 - 27 July 1755 Nicholas Broadaway, Carpenter, to Thomas Ringgold of Chester Town, Kent County (Md.), Gentleman - consideration Ŀ72 current money - 62 acres of land called "White Hall" - lying near Collins' Mill and the old church - the line intersecting a tract called "Churnell" - purchased of John Hollingsworth. Also 38 acres, part of "Notley's Desire," adjoining "White Hall" and the main road, about one-half mile from the head of the Southeast Branch, bought of Richard Flinn - a mortgage due on or before 10 November next. Acknowledged before James Brown and Dowdall Thompson.

319. ADVERTISEMENT. 26 July 1755 - 31 July 1755 Taken up as a stray by Edward Skinner near the Horsehead and brought before me, a black mare with a young colt - branded. Dowdall Thompson.

319. 30 July 1755 - 31 July 1755 ADVERTISEMENT. Taken up as a stray by Samuel Massey at the Chester Town Ferry, a bay mare, neither dock't nor branded, has lost her eye on the off side. Dowdall Thompson.

319. 23 August 1755 - 27 August 1755 Edward Clayton, Gentleman, to James Ringgold of Eastern Neck, Kent County (Md.), Gentleman - in exchange with Ringgold of nine acres of land, part of two tracts on the north side of Coursica Creek, called "Coursey's Point" and "Brampton's Addition" - conveyed to Ringgold part of "Bishop's Addition," containing nine acres of land. Wit: George Garnett, Solomon Wright. Acknowledged before Richard Tilghman, Justice of the Provincial Court. Alienation fine, four pence, half penny sterling.

320. 3 June 1755 - 28 August 1755 John Chairs, Planter, to John Vanderford, Planter - consideration Ŀ100 current money and 5,000 pounds of tobacco - part of "Wrench'es Farm" - lying on or near the head of Robotham's Branch - lately by deed dated 31 October 1741 given by William Wrench the elder, of St. Paul's Parish (Queen Ann's County), to his daughter Margarett, the wife of James Chairs and on 5 May 1750 by Margarett, then widow of James Chairs conveyed to John Chairs - all of the farm on the north side of Robotham's Branch - adjoining "Vineyard." John and Ann his wife (she being first privately examined out of his hearing) acknowledged before Jonathon Nicols and John Bracco.

321. 6 September 1755 - 11 September 1755 William Tilghman, Gentleman, to Matthew Tilghman of Talbot County, Gentleman - consideration Ŀ300 current money of the Province - 191 acres, part of "Poplar Plain" and part of "Delmorend," in the branches at the head of Chester River - adjoining "Tilghman's Forest" - "Delmorend" contains 150 acres. Wit: James Tilghman, Edward Pryce Wilmer. William and Margaret his wife (she being first privately examined) acknowledged before Richard Tilghman, Justice of the Provincial Court. Alienation fine, thirteen shillings, eight pence sterling.

323. 13 September 1755 Deed Tripartite - between Ann Jacobs, widow, Thomas Baker, Gentleman, and John Atkinson. In anticipation of a marriage to take place between Ann Jacobs and Thomas Baker, John

323. Atkinson is appointed trustee to insure the conditions of their marriage contract - the details given. Wit: Richard Tilghman, Richard Skinner. Acknowledged before Richard Tilghman, Justice of the Provincial Court.

324. 12 September 1755 - 13 September 1755 Joseph Jermin, Planter, to William Cannon - in consideration of £9.5.3 current money and 19,267½ pounds of tobacco paid by him to Coll. Edward Lloyd for my debts - one negro man; one negro woman; seven sheep; seventeen hogs; a parcel of cyder casks; two featherbeds and furniture; seven cattle; one gray mare; one bay mare; one plow and tackling; one pair of pistols and holsters; one iron pottrack and one iron pott and all the tobacco in bulk to strip in the tobacco house and all crops of tobacco and Indian corn now growing on the ground and one pair iron pothooks. Wit: William Lundergin, William Goldsborough. Acknowledged before John Bracco. (Jermin also written "Jarmon.")

325. 12 May 1755 - 13 September 1755 Joseph Jarman to his daughter, Alice Cannon, wife of William Cannon the younger - in consideration of the love and affection borne to her - a negro boy about four years of age, named "Young London." Wit: Sarah Walker, N. Wright.

326. 20 August 1755 - 13 September 1755 Joseph Jarman, Planter, to his daughter, Sarah Jarman - a negro girl named "Franck," about four years of age. Sarah agreed not to sell or mortgage the girl before her marriage. Wit: Thomas Marsh, William Cannon.

326. 1 September 1755 - 17 September 1755 John Merrick, Planter, to William Banckes, Merchant - consideration £30 current money of the Province - 50 acres of land in the Forrest of Choptank, called "Merrick's Delight." Acknowledged before Jonathon Nicols and John Bracco. Alienation fine, two shillings sterling, paid to Richard Tilghman.

327. ADVERTISEMENT. 15 September 1755 - 17 September 1755 Taken up as a stray by Joseph Slocom near Thomas Hamer's - a middling size bay horse - the owner proving his property and paying costs can claim. Dowdall Thompson.

327. 18 August 1755 - 17 September 1755 John Falconer, Planter, to John Hall, Planter - consideration £20.9.6 current money - 21½ acres of land called "Falkner's Hope" - lying between "Welch Poole" and "Hog Harbour" and near the French Woman's Branch - adjoining "Hogg Harbour" now in the possession of John Hall and on the southeast side of the road to Worley's Bridge from the Golden Bridge. John and Mary his wife (she being first privately examined out of his hearing) acknowledged before Jonathon Nicols and John Bracco. Alienation fine, ten pence, half penny sterling.

328. 1 September 1775 - 18 September 1755 John Whitby, Planter, and Deborah his wife, to Benjamin Silvester, Planter - consideration 3,500 pounds of tobacco - 76 acres, "Hemsly's Dispute" - lying near

328. White Rump's Pond and on the north side of the road from Choptank Bridge to Tuckahoe Bridge. John and Deborah his wife (she being first privately examined) acknowledged before Jonathon Nicols and John Bracco. Alienation fine, three shillings, two pence sterling.

330. 31 March 1755 - 19 September 1755 Joseph Jackson, Planter, to Vincent Benton, Planter - consideration ₤128 current money - 200 acres of land called "Jesper's Lott" - lying on the west side of the little Red Lyon Branch - according to a deed made to Thomas Jackson and Barbery his wife from John Hawkins - adjoining the land of John Davis. Joseph and Ann his wife (she being first privately examined) acknowledged before Nathan Wright and Dowdall Thompson. Alienation fine, eight shillings sterling, paid to Richard Tilghman.

331. 23 June 1755 - 19 September 1755 John Andrews of Salem, County of Salem, Province of New Jersey, Yoeman, to Stephen Andrews, Planter - consideration ₤30 current money of New Jersey - 50 acres of land in Queen Ann's County, called "Mount Gilboa" - according to the original survey. John Nevill and William Ponder, Planters, appointed attorneys to acknowledge the deed for John Andrews. Wit: John Humphry, Thomas Rice. Acknowledged before James Brown and Dowdall Thompson. Alienation fine, two shillings sterling.

332. 19 August 1755 - 19 September 1755 Joshua Wollaston to Joshua Vansant and John Blackiston of Kent County, Province of Maryland - to secure a bond made 30 April 1755 in the amount of ₤222 - conveys Robass'es Mill on Red Lyon Branch - sold by Thomas Ringgold to Joshua Wollaston. Acknowledged before James Brown and Dowdall Thompson.

333. 2 October 1755 Matthew Chilton, Planter, and Mary his wife, to George Porter of Talbot County - consideration ₤35 current - "New Cumming," 100 acres lying between Choptank River and Tuckahoe Creek in the woods - adjoining "Jump's Choice," formerly laid out for William Jump - on Jones' Path. Wit: Richard Tilghman, Stead Lowe. Matthew and Mary his wife (she being first privately examined) acknowledged before Richard Tilghman, Justice of the Provincial Court.

334. 17 October 1755 Thomas Richardson Roe, Planter, to John Tillotson - consideration 6,000 pounds of tobacco and ₤35 current money - two featherbeds and furniture that is good, Wilshire ruggs, blankets, sheets, bolster and pillow, bedstead and cord; thirty hogs; six cattle; six sheep; two mares; one dozen and five plates; five sortable dishes; one chester (sic!) drawers; one old glass; one old negro woman named "Bess." Acknowledged before Richard Tilghman.

335. 26 July 1755 - 25 October 1755 Abraham McCassley, Planter, to John Seegar, Planter - consideration 4,000 pounds of tobacco - 62 acres of land called "Forkalet" - adjoining "Green's Hazard" on Green Swamp Branch. Abraham and Sarah his wife (she being first privately examined) acknowledged before James Brown and Dowdall Thompson. Alienation fine, two shillings, six pence sterling.

336. 10 November 1755 Thomas Wilkinson the Elder, Planter, John Wilkinson, Thomas Wilkinson the Younger and Christopher Wilkinson, Planters, son of Thomas, to John Jackson, Physician - consideration ₤400 current money - 350 acres, "Barbadoes Hall." - A mortgage due on or before 10 November 1760. Wit: Richard Tilghman, Alexander Williamson, Jr. Acknowledged before Richard Tilghman, Justice of the Provincial Court.

338. 27 September 1755 - 13 November 1755 William Ridgway, Planter, and Mary his wife, to Mary Jolley - consideration ₤16 current money - 50 acres of land called "Hope" - lying between Unicorn and Andover Branches. William and Mary his wife (she being first privately examined out of his hearing) acknowledged before James Brown and Dowdall Thompson.

339. 13 November 1755 Charles Seth, Carpenter, to Dennis Carey, Planter - consideration ₤12 current money - 15 acres of land, part of "Bennett's Outlet" - near the head of Back Wye River - adjoining "Forsett's Plains." Charles and Rachel his wife (she being first privately examined) acknowledged before William Tilghman and John Downes, Jr. Alienation fine, seven pence, half penny sterling.

340. 13 November 1755 Dennis Cary to Charles Seth, Carpenter - consideration 2,450 pounds of tobacco, ₤12 current money of Maryland, and four shillings sterling money of Great Britain - 40 acres of land, part of "Middle Plantation" - adjoining "Addition" and "Mt. Mill." Dennis and Sarah his wife (she being first privately examined) acknowledged before William Tilghman and John Downes, Jr. Alienation fine, one shilling, eight pence sterling.

341. 17 September 1755 - 21 November 1755 John Scott, Planter, to Edward Lloyd, Esquire, of Talbot County - consideration 30,000 pounds of tobacco - 532½ acres of land, part of "Stratton" - lying on the west side of Tuckahoe Creek - a mortgage due within three years of date. Wit: Philemon Lloyd Chew, William Geddes. John and Anne his wife (she being first privately examined) acknowledged before Jonathon Nicols and John Bracco.

343. 11 September 1755 - 20 November 1755 James Ponder, Planter, and Elizabeth his wife, to James McCoy, Cordwinder - consideration ₤20 current money - 38 acres of land called "Ponder's Chance" - lying near the head of Double Creek - adjoining "Smith's Delight." James and Elizabeth (she being first privately examined) acknowledged before James Brown and Dowdall Thompson.

345. ADVERTISEMENT. 24 November 1755 - 25 November 1755 Taken up as a stray by Solomon Wyate, near the Red Lyon Branch, a black horse of middling size (no brand perceived) - any person owning him may have of Solomon Wyate, proving his property and paying charges. Dowdall Thompson.

345. 25 November 1755 Benjamin Denny, Planter, and Susanna his wife, to

345. Stephen Gudgeon, Schoolmaster - consideration ₺25 current money - 50 acres of land, part of the "Outlet." Benjamin and Susanna (she being first privately examined out of hearing of her husband) acknowledged before Nathan Wright and John Downes, Jr. Alienation fine, two shillings sterling, paid to Richard Tilghman.

346. 13 September 1755 - 25 November 1755 Edward Jones, Planter, and Elizabeth his wife, to Farintine Jackson, daughter of Edward Jones and now wife of John Jackson - a gift of love - 30 acres of land called "Ford's Park," whereon John Jackson now dwells - also 30 acres, part of "Nottingham," adjoining. Edward and Elizabeth (she being first privately examined) acknowledged before James Brown and Dowdall Thompson. Alienation fine, two shillings, five pence sterling.

347. 26 November 1755 John Thorpe of Kent County, Delaware, to Isaac Thorpe, Planter - consideration ₺15 current - 50 acres, part of "Colerain" - adjoining Croney and Ross's lands and on the road leading from Worley's Bridge to Tuckahoe Bridge - bequeathed by James Jordan to his son John Jordan. John and Elizabeth his wife (she being first privately examined) acknowledged before John Downes, Jr. and John Bracco. Alienation fine, one shilling sterling.

348. 18 August 1755 - 26 November 1755 Richard Nicholas of Cecill County (Md.), Millwright, to Joshua Wollaston - consideration ₺110 current money - his part of twenty acres and the improvements thereon, lying on the Red Lyon Branch - parts of two tracts of land, one is called "Condon" and the other, "Crompton" - sold by James Robass, Millwright, to Daniel Cheston and by Thomas Ringgold, attorney, to Joshua Wollaston of New Castle County, Innholder, and the aforesaid Richard Nicholas - with all houses, mills, mill wheels, mill stones, tackle, furniture and apparell to the mill belonging. Acknowledged before James Brown and Dowdall Thompson.

350. 29 November 1755 - 28 November 1755 Samuel Hunt of Hunterdon County, Government of New Jersey, to John Brown - one roan mare about four years of age - for the consideration of one bay gelding and ₺5 current money. Acknowledged before Dowdall Thompson.

350. 11 November 1755 - 29 November 1755 Thomas Teat, Planter, to John Nevil, Planter - consideration ₺35 current money - 50 acres called the "Bee Tree Ridge," in the Forrest of Choptank on Chicken Marsh, part of Long Marsh - in trust for the heirs of Sarah Johnson, wife of John Johnson of "Ripply," late of Queen Ann's County - after the death of Sarah, Nevil to convey 50 acres to Mary, daughter of the said Sarah and in case of Mary's death, to John Johnson, son of the said Sarah. Thomas Teat and Sarah his wife (she being first privately examined out of his hearing) acknowledged before James Brown and Dowdall Thompson. Alienation fine, two shillings sterling.

352. 8 September 1755 - 29 November 1755 John Roe, Planter, eldest son

352. of Thomas Roe, deceased, to Joseph Roe, Blacksmith - a lease of 70 acres of land called "Roe's Addition," adjoining "Downes'es Forrest" and 60 acres, part of "Downes'es Forrest," adjoining "Roe's Addition" - all delivered by John Roe, grandfather of the said John Roe, since deceased, according to his will, written 17 June 1736. The rent, ₤2 per annum. Wit: John Marsh, Samuel Roe, Thomas Richardson Roe.

353. 25 November 1755 - 29 November 1755 William Hunter, Planter, to Ezekial Hunter, Planter - consideration ₤10 current money - 100 acres of land, part of "Hunter's Levels" - on the east side of Tuckahoe Creek - adjoining "Boon's Ridge." William and Rebecca his wife (she being first privately examined) acknowledged their deed before John Downes, Jr. and John Bracco. Alienation fine, two shillings sterling, paid to Richard Tilghman.

354. 20 August 1755 - 1 December 1755 George Millington of Talbot County, Planter, and Hannah his wife, to Henry Casson, Merchant - consideration 7,000 pounds of tobacco - one-third of "Pitts' Vineyard," on the east side of Tuckahoe Creek (bequeathed to Hannah by Thomas Baynard of Talbot County, her late husband, and part of a deed of partition made between John Baynard, the same Thomas Baynard, and John Baynard, son of William Baynard - containing 166 2/3 acres. George and Hannah (she being first privately examined out of his hearing) acknowledged before Jonathon Nicols and John Bracco. Alienation fine, six shillings, eight pence sterling.

356. 1 December 1755 Solomon Jumpe, Planter, to William Banckes, Merchant - consideration 1,000 pounds of tobacco and ₤35 current money - 93 acres of land, part of "Pokety Ridge," part of "Jump's Chance" and part of "Jump's Addition" (whereon I now dwell) - a mortgage, due by 30 December 1758. Acknowledged before Jonathon Nicols and John Bracco.

Here ends Volume R. T. D 1751 - 1755

QUEEN ANNE COUNTY, MARYLAND, LAND RECORDS

INDEX TO VOLUME R. T. C 1743 - 1751

NOTE:
The names and titles appearing in the Patent and Rent Roll records on page 46 are not included in this index.

QUEEN ANNE COUNTY, MARYLAND, LAND RECORDS

INDEX TO VOLUME R. T. D 1751 - 1755

Printed by
THE ANUNDSEN PUBLISHING CO.
108 Washington Street
Decorah, Iowa 52101

Heritage Books by R. Bernice Leonard

Queen Anne's County, Maryland Land Records, Book 1: 1701–1725

Queen Anne's County, Maryland Land Records, Book 2: 1725–1741

Queen Anne's County, Maryland Land Records, Book 3: 1738–1747

Queen Anne's County, Maryland Land Records, Book 4: 1743–1755

Talbot County, Maryland Land Records, Book 1: 1662–1675

Talbot County, Maryland Land Records, Book 2: 1676–1691

Talbot County, Maryland Land Records, Book 3: 1692–1702

Talbot County, Maryland Land Records, Book 4: 1702–1712

Talbot County, Maryland Land Records, Book 5: 1712–1725

Talbot County, Maryland Land Records, Book 6: 1725–1733

Talbot County, Maryland Land Records, Book 7: 1733–1740

Talbot County, Maryland Land Records, Book 8: 1740–1745

Talbot County, Maryland Land Records, Book 9: 1745–1751

Talbot County, Maryland Land Records, Book 10: 1751–1758

Talbot County, Maryland Land Records, Book 11: 1758–1765

Talbot County, Maryland Land Records, Book 12: 1765–1771

Talbot County, Maryland Land Records, Book 13: 1771–1777

Talbot County, Maryland Land Records, Book 14: 1777–1784

Talbot County, Maryland Land Records, Book 15: 1784–1790

www.ingramcontent.com/pod-product-compliance
Lightning Source LLC
Chambersburg PA
CBHW072153270326
41930CB00011B/2415